S0-ATS-541

Things Remembered and Things Forgotten

Things Remembered and Things Forgotten

KYOKO NAKAJIMA

Translated from the Japanese by

IAN MCCULLOUGH MACDONALD
and GINNY TAPLEY TAKEMORI

First published in Great Britain in 2021 by
Sort Of Books
PO Box 18678, London NW3 2FL
www.sortof.co.uk

Stories © Kyoko Nakajima, 2021

English translations

© Ian McCullough MacDonald, 2021
*Things Remembered and Things Forgotten, Global Positioning System,
Kirara's Paper Plane, Childhood Friends, The Last Obon*

© Ginny Tapley Takemori, 2021
*When My Wife Was a Shiitake, The Life Story of a Sewing Machine, A
Special Day, The Pet Civet, The Harajuku House*

ISBN 978-1908745965
e-ISBN 978-1908745972

Typeset in Goudy Old Style to a design by Henry Iles.

Printed and bound in Great Britain by Clays Ltd, Elcograf S.p.A.

Contents

Things Remembered
and Things Forgotten

MASARU MASAOKA, in the passenger seat of the silver
Lexus, sneezed nervously. His wife Yumi was driving, and
they were on the western outskirts of Tokyo.

'Must be the autumn pollen – lots of ragweed out here
in the sticks. Put up the windows, will you?' he said.

Yumi pressed the power window switch, and Masaru
tilted his seat back, shutting his eyes.

'Are you going to take a nap?'

'I'm not sleepy. Anyway, we'll be there soon.'

'You know, dear, we haven't seen your brother in
almost forty years. Not since our wedding. I'm feeling a
little awkward.'

'You shouldn't. It's not like he's ever expressed any
desire to see us. And, considering his condition' –
Masaru paused and tapped his temple with his index
finger – 'he probably won't even recognise me.'

They crossed a bridge and turned off the highway onto
a narrow road. Soon they arrived at their destination: a
single-family house remodelled to serve as a group home
for the elderly. The Masaokas were shown through to

the lounge where a man sat watching television and four women were gathered around a table folding pieces of fabric. Two other women sat dozing, each in her own chair, their bodies slumped to one side or the other. Just then a thin elderly man came shuffling in.

'Takashi,' Masaru called out.

The man responded with a friendly salute and a bow. The women at the table stopped what they were doing and bowed politely.

'Takashi, it's me, Masaru. You remember Yumi.'

'I'm sorry we haven't seen you for so long,' said Yumi, bowing deeply to her husband's elder brother, who nodded his head and smiled.

Everything in the room – from the artlessly arranged cabinets to the kokeshi dolls and knick-knacks inside them – were of considerable antiquity, just like the home's human occupants.

'This really takes you back, doesn't it, Takashi?'

In response to Masaru's remark, a staff member volunteered that the home was equipped with all the latest modern conveniences, including an elevator and newly remodelled bathrooms. But, he said, the furniture, paintings and other items had been deliberately chosen to evoke an 'old-time' atmosphere.

'It makes our patrons feel at home,' explained the staff member. 'And, just between you and me, I picked these things up for a song at a thrift shop.'

Masaru took his brother's arm and led him over to the window, then pulled open the lace curtain.

'This takes me back, too,' Masaru said.

The window looked out onto a floodplain where children were playing baseball, the wide Tama River flowing by. Masaru's brother sat down in an armchair nearby. 'There's a bird,' he said to no one in particular.

'You're right. How unusual. Is it an egret? It *is*, isn't it? Hey, Takashi, doesn't it remind you of Tsukishima? Doesn't it?' Masaru felt a wave of nostalgia washing over him.

But his elder brother was absorbed in the graceful white bird that had alighted at the river's edge, seemingly uninterested in any distant memory. He moved his head up and down as though he were tracing the bird's movements with his chin.

Yumi broke in. 'I didn't know you and Takashi had lived in Tsukishima.'

'Yes. A long, long time ago.'

'You never told me that.'

'Didn't I? Maybe not. It was nearly seventy years ago.'

'We should have asked Takashi to come visit us there – for old times' sake.'

'That's a laugh. Nothing but high-rise apartment buildings there now. This place is more like Tsukishima was in those days.'

'I suppose you're right.' Yumi shrugged her shoulders.

'Are you getting tired, Takashi?' Masaru spoke, more loudly now, into his elder brother's ear.

'Yes. I suppose I am.'

TAKASHI SET OFF, leading his little brother by the hand. At the end of the narrow alley lined with flowerpots, they came to the grassy expanse alongside the Sumida

River. To their left they could see the huge Kachidoki Drawbridge opening and closing.

Beyond it, across the river, stood the hospital requisitioned by the Occupation Army and Hongan-ji with its Indian-style main temple hall. Straight ahead, across Mihara Bridge, stood the old clock tower building in Ginza that now served as the military PX. Takashi, who was eight, and Masaru, who was three, had heard that there were lots of American GIs there who handed out chocolates and chewing gum to children. But their mother had warned them: 'Don't go near the drawbridge or the GIs will grab you and line you up for target practice.' So they had never crossed the river.

The bridge was used by American soldiers going to the PX or GHQ from their barracks in Harumi, on the east side of Tsukishima ('where the World's Fair would've been if it hadn't been for the war', people muttered), and was said to be teeming with drunk GIs who caused all kinds of trouble. So whenever Takashi's mother suggested he take Masaru outside, they headed either west to the river to stare off towards Ginza, or north across the scorched grassland that Tsukuda had become, to sit at the foot of Aioi Bridge.

As Takashi and Masaru returned to their neighbourhood dotted with the skeletons of burned-out houses, a sudden gust of wind knocked over the washboard and bucket that had been left out to dry. The bucket came hurtling towards the smaller boy. Takashi jerked his brother out of the way, and Masaru spun, pivoting on one foot with his arm above his head like a young woman in a dance hall twirling in the arms of her beau.

Masaru was wearing baggy trousers, hand-me-downs from his big brother. Takashi's were too short and had been worn for so long they were tattered and threadbare.

'Back so soon?' said the old lady who lived on the first floor, peering over spectacles perched on her nose. 'Well, come in and sit with me, boys. Your ma's not home yet.'

Takashi nodded, urging his little brother forwards, and together they went in and plopped themselves down in a corner of the small sitting room.

The old lady turned to the gasman who had come about a leaky valve. 'You lied to me last month,' she said.

'How so?' replied the man, fiddling with the rubber hose.

'You said since Japan surrendered "unconditionally", the Americans wouldn't take our land or force Japan to pay reparations. Because it was "unconditional". That's what you said. Now look at all that land across the river they've gone and taken.'

'It hasn't been *taken*,' said the man, who was in his late fifties. 'It's just been requisitioned.'

The old lady tilted her head to one side, repeating *rek-we-zish-und* under her breath. She didn't understand the meaning of the word any more than she knew what 'unconditional surrender' meant, and in truth the gasman didn't either. He replaced the old gas hose with a new one and left the old lady frowning at the receipt.

'My,' she said, clicking her tongue, 'what things cost these days!'

No sooner had the gasman left than the boys' young mother slid open the front door.

'How'd it go?' asked the old lady.

'Bad – really bad,' Tomiyo replied, waving her hand emphatically over her head. 'It wasn't what I expected at all. I couldn't believe it.'

'In what way?'

'In every way. I was completely floored.'

Kneeling down on the tatami, Tomiyo reached over and gave each of her sons a pat on the head. 'Did you two behave yourselves?' she asked. 'I'll steam some sweet potatoes for you later.'

'This is what I went to see about,' she said, seating herself on a cushion at the low dining table and smoothing the curled edges of something she'd cut out from the newspaper.

She read aloud to the old lady:

URGENTLY SEEKING QUALIFIED FEMALE STAFF
Excellent pay and benefits – food, clothing and
lodging provided; salary payable in advance upon
request. Will reimburse applicants' travel expenses
from anywhere in Japan.

'Sounds too good to be true, doesn't it? Well, when I told them I had two kids they told me this work was unsuitable for married women.'

'Smells fishy if you ask me,' said the old lady.

'Yeah, *real* fishy!' Tomiyo replied, pinching her nose. 'I should've consulted you before going. Want to know what they asked me? "Are you prepared to serve as a sexual breakwater to protect and nurture the purity of our race for the next hundred years?" Imagine!'

The old lady – comprehending this even less than she understood 'unconditional surrender' – gave the younger woman the blank look of a Noh mask.

Tomiyo frowned and shook her head. 'In other words, you know...' She paused and glanced at her two boys. 'Doing *it* – with American GIs. Can you believe it? I was in shock. I ran straight out of there.'

'Did they pay your travel expenses at least?'

Tomiyo shook her head again. Just then she noticed a small child with a runny nose standing outside the front door.

'Who's that boy?'

'No idea. He's been hanging around since morning.'

'Looks about the same age as Masaru.'

'WELL, SO LONG, TAKASHI. We'll come again.'

Masaru Masaoka rested a hand on his elder brother's shoulder. Takashi patted it several times.

'Take care of yourself, Takashi.'

Together Masaru and Yumi walked towards the front door. Takashi, shuffling from the lounge, softly called out Masaru's name.

'What is it?' Masaru asked, turning around.

Takashi just smiled and waved.

The Masaokas bowed to the staff and walked to their car. 'Your brother remembered you, dear. He said your name.'

'Some things you remember, others you forget.'

Masaru took the car keys from his wife and climbed into the driver's seat of the Lexus.

'Well, well. This is a change.'

'What is?'

'You driving – and taking a day off, for that matter. I never expected you to be so busy in your retirement.'

'What did you think? I'm learning a new job. It takes time to get up to speed.'

'Is it going well? It's so different from what you used to do.'

'Yeah, well, I was in the wrong field before. After all, I studied humanities, remember?'

'So why did you stay at the power company for forty years?'

'Back then the best and brightest were all going into nuclear energy, even if you didn't have a science background. That's just the way things were.'

'Where was it your brother worked?'

'Why do you always make a point of asking me that?'

'Do I?'

'You do. He dropped out of school after junior high and got a job in a factory. I don't remember where he ended up. A small book bindery or someplace like that.'

'I can never remember – not unless I have a name to latch on to.'

'Not everyone works for a blue-chip company like in your family.'

Feeling slightly chastised, Yumi shifted her gaze out the window. They were stuck in a traffic jam on the

Chuo Expressway and had only got as far as the turn-off for Chofu Airport.

'When did you and Takashi live in Tsukishima?'

Yumi took a sip from a bottle of green tea and placed it in the cup holder behind the gearstick. Masaru reached over and grabbed the bottle.

'Want a sip?' She took the bottle from him and unscrewed the cap, then handed it back to her husband.

'Let's see. Not that long. We went there to stay with a family friend when the air raids got really bad. I must've been two at the time, not that I remember. Then the year after the war ended, we moved to Chiba.'

'Your father fought in the South Pacific?'

'Yeah, but he never came back – not even his ashes.'

'You were twelve when your mother died, right? So Takashi would have been seventeen.'

'Sounds about right.' Masaru took a sip of tea, then muttered, 'An accident – so that's what it was.' Once they passed the scene of the crash, the traffic started to flow again.

'I suppose he looked after you most of the time growing up.'

'Are you kidding? I looked after *him*. Takashi was kind of a screw-up. He did badly at school. Always near the bottom of his class.'

'And I suppose you were near the top?'

'Not *near*.'

'What? Oh, meaning you were *first* in your class? You shouldn't brag, dear – that's what annoys Masato.'

'I guess Masato takes after Takashi, then.'

'*Really*, dear. Don't start!' said Yumi. 'So how long did you and your brother live together?'

'He moved into the factory dormitory the year I graduated from junior high.'

'And you lived with your aunt and uncle in Chiba while you went to high school ... I know the rest by heart.'

'Those were the good old days. It didn't matter if you were poor. So long as you had brains, there were plenty of opportunities.'

'Please don't go into that all over again,' said Yumi, rolling her eyes. 'Did you see Takashi often?'

'From time to time.'

'Such as when?'

'Weddings, death anniversaries – that sort of thing.'

'He didn't come to either your aunt's or uncle's funerals.'

'Didn't he? Well, brothers are like that.'

'You know, I don't think Takashi is as senile as you think, dear.'

'How so?'

'He knew exactly who you were.'

'Memories come back when you see someone face to face.'

'He's been alone all his life.'

'Since his wife died, anyway. That was before you and I were married. Look, I'm not as heartless as you make me sound. I chose that home carefully after talking to the long-term care manager.'

'Which way are you going, dear?' asked Yumi, glancing at her husband. They had come to the Hamazakibashi Junction and he had headed off to the right.

'Darn. I didn't mean to do that. It's because I haven't driven for so long.'

'I'm glad even you make mistakes sometimes. Isn't this fun!'

'Fun – how so?'

'It's a nice day. Let's take the Rainbow Bridge over to Toyosu and go home that way. It's not much longer, anyway.'

'Wow, this area has completely changed.'

'Has it?'

'None of these buildings were here before.'

'You mean when you lived in Tsukishima with your brother?'

'Yeah.'

'Well, things change. Anyway, do you really remember? You were so little at the time.'

'I remember. Better than Takashi, anyway.'

'Do you? You've forgot a lot of things. Things from before we were married.'

'Don't be ridiculous.'

'Some things you remember, others you forget – isn't that what you said?'

ON ANOTHER DAY, Takashi took his little brother to Aioi Bridge. It was autumn and the tall grasses along the riverbank were turning brown and smelling wonderful. Takashi took a deep breath, filling his lungs with the cool air, and ran through the grass with his arms spread wide, making a droning sound. 'Brrrrrr.'

Masaru ran along behind, mimicking him. He copied everything Takashi did.

'Brrrrr,' he droned in his high voice.

The next moment Takashi cried out in alarm. Masaru was no longer running behind him. He'd tripped and was rolling down the embankment. Takashi broke into a cold sweat as he imagined his brother ending up in the water. But just then, with a thud, Masaru collided into another child.

It was the same little boy who had been hanging around outside their house all morning. Takashi looked fiercely at the boy but gave up and went back to running around with his arms outstretched, droning like an airplane. Masaru started running again, too, in imitation, and then the other little boy took up the game as well, until all three were running around and going, 'Brrrrr.' The boys played like that until the sun went down. There was nothing else for them to do.

At dusk the two brothers returned to their cramped neighbourhood of ramshackle terraced houses to find that the old lady's granddaughter had dropped by with some canned meats and fruits.

'I've applied for a job as a maid in one of the requisitioned houses,' said the young woman, who was wearing a bright-coloured dress.

'Are you crazy?' said her grandmother angrily. 'You mustn't take a job like that. What will you do if something happens? "Science for boys, etiquette for girls" – that's the motto these days. A woman has to guard her virginity.'

'Don't worry, Grandma. It's for a married couple. They've even got kids.'

'But don't you have to be able to speak English?' asked Tomiyo, a bit childishly.

'Not really. All I need to do is keep saying "Yes, sir" and "Yes, ma'am". It's a great big mansion in Ookayama. I met the husband today. He wants me to start next month after his wife and kids arrive. Then I'll be able to bring you jam and canned food all the time, Grandma.'

'Sounds too good to be true if you ask me.'

'It isn't. You'll see,' said the girl smugly.

Tomiyo sighed. 'Perhaps I should take English typing lessons or something,' she said uncertainly.

'What for?' asked the girl.

'Every day the newspaper's full of help-wanted ads for people who can type in English.'

'Don't bother with lessons – just go ahead and apply.'

'But nobody will hire me unless I can type.'

'Just act like you know what you're doing. You'll pick it up as you go along, even if you have to hunt and peck at first.'

'I suppose so.' Tomiyo stared down at her fingers dubiously.

From the entryway came the sound of the front door opening, and in stepped the upstairs lodger. He was leading a little boy by the hand.

'And what do we have here?' asked the old lady suspiciously, a proprietary tone in her voice.

'I found him wandering around outside,' the lodger said. 'Since it's late I thought he could stay here tonight. In the morning I'll take him over to the police station.'

'I've seen him before – he's been hanging around here a lot.'

'I can't get much out of him. Maybe he's lost or maybe his parents are dead.'

Just then the two brothers, noticing the boy, called out to him.

'Do you know him?' asked the lodger.

The boys nodded.

'Where's he live?'

They both shook their heads. The little boy rushed over to his new playmates.

'All right, he can stay,' said Tomiyo, on behalf of the old lady. 'But just for tonight.'

'Hey,' said the lodger, changing the topic, 'about that job you were just talking about – I think you should give it a go.'

'You see?' said the girl, pleased with herself.

'As a matter of fact, I found something in the newspaper too. Take a look.' The lodger slipped his hand into his trouser pocket and took out a clipping for Tomiyo to read.

The editors of *Bungei Shunju* request that anyone who has ever contributed a story to our magazine contact our offices and let us know your current address. We would also be glad to receive news about how you are doing.

'Their records must've been destroyed in the war,' explained the lodger. 'I was thinking of contacting them and trying to sell them a story.'

'Ha!' interjected a second lodger, an ex-soldier, who was standing in the entryway listening to the conversation. 'Good luck with that. Records or no records, a magazine editor can tell the difference between a writer and a wannabe.'

'But,' protested the would-be writer, 'it says "anyone who has *ever* contributed a story" to the magazine.'

'Yeah, it doesn't say "anyone who has *never* contributed a story".'

'There isn't much difference between "ever" and "never".'

The ex-soldier didn't bother replying. He lowered a sack from his shoulder and placed it before the old lady.

'You're too kind!' The old lady beamed.

'It's just some sweet potatoes. A contact got them for me,' he said.

'So how's business?'

'Not bad.' He massaged his shoulder. 'Things have picked up since I started selling those pictures of Mount Fuji.'

'That's great,' chimed in Tomiyo. In addition to her work sewing clothes by the piece, she made paper fans, which the ex-soldier, a struggling artist, painted with scenes of Mount Fuji and sold to souvenir shops catering to American soldiers.

A strong gust of wind buffeted the front door, rattling the glass.

'Lot of typhoons this year,' said the would-be writer.

'Yeah, but where was all that "divine wind" when we needed it?' the ex-soldier said sarcastically.

'But it did come. They say the divine wind delayed the Americans' arrival by two or three days.'

'Really? A lot of good *that* did.'

'It bought the authorities enough time to destroy a bunch of documents they didn't want the Americans to get their hands on.'

The old lady nodded seriously. 'That's what all that ash was,' she said.

TOWARDS THE END of the year in which the war ended, Masaru died.

He caught a cold that turned into pneumonia, and he was too malnourished to recover.

It was something Takashi remembered but Masaru had forgotten.

Takashi and his mother cried all winter long. They were still crying when the little boy, the playmate of the two brothers, reappeared at their door.

Takashi quietly slipped his hand into the little boy's and led him inside.

When My Wife
Was a Shiitake

Omwet.
No, no. Omelette.
Omwet.
Not omwet, omelette.
Omwet. Omwet?
What about this?
Sweet.
Sweet? And this?
Green.
Green, is it? Well, what about this?
Clam.
That's right, clam. And this?
Shiitako.
Almost – shiitake.
Shiitake.

ON A COLD DAY seven years ago, just two days into his retirement, Taihei's wife died. When she still wasn't up at noon, he'd gone to the bedroom to wake her, cracking a joke – *Is this how lazy you get when the head of the household doesn't have to go to work any more?* – only to find that her heart had stopped beating. An ambulance took her away, and the cause of death was diagnosed as a subarachnoid haemorrhage. The night before she'd complained of not feeling herself and had gone to bed ahead of him, he recalled, but it had never occurred to him she would die just like that.

The funeral had come and gone in the blink of an eye, with no time to grieve. Two or three weeks later, when the number of visitors had dwindled, Taihei was sitting all alone in a daze one night when his daughter, who lived in Tokyo, called.

'I just remembered that the cooking class with Tomiko Sugiyama is tomorrow. It's really popular and cancellations aren't allowed, so why don't you go instead?'

'What are you talking about?' Taihei asked in his stupor.

'Oh come on, don't you know? It's the cooking class. The one Mum applied for. She was really looking forward to it. Getting into a class with Tomiko Sugiyama for her was like winning the lottery. She's already paid for it, you know.'

'That's more your sort of thing.'

'I'd love to go, but I've got work. You haven't got anything planned for tomorrow, have you, Dad? You should go. It'll help take your mind off things.'

'I can't cook.'

'That's a good reason to go, isn't it? After all, it's a cooking class.'

'Not for me, it isn't. Give me her number and I'll call to give her our apologies.'

'You'd be better off just going to it, though.' Her voice on the other end of the line sounded irritable. 'Look, Dad, you're going to have to do everything for yourself from now on. Think of it as a first step.'

'Just give me the number.'

'I think it's in Mum's address book. But you can't turn it down, you know. It's unheard of for anyone to cancel a class with Tomiko Sugiyama.'

'Whoever heard of not being able to cancel a cooking class for someone who's died?' Taihei retorted caustically. He hung up and located the number, recorded meticulously in his wife's address book.

'Tomiko Sugiyama's Cooking Class. How can I help you?' said a voice brightly on the other end of the line.

'I'm calling on behalf of Misako Ishida, who was due to come to your class tomorrow. I'm her husband,' he started, but the bright voice cut in, cheerfully taking charge of the conversation.

'Oh, Mr Ishida, thank you for calling. Your daughter contacted me earlier. I'm looking forward to seeing you tomorrow.'

'I beg your pardon?'

'As I mentioned to your daughter, all you need to bring with you is some salty-sweet shiitake, ready prepared.'

'What?'

'Just some shiitake, simmered in sugar and soy sauce.'

'No, no, the thing is, my wife had a brain haemorrhage the other day.'

'Indeed.' The owner of the bright voice paused, as if struggling between a desire to express her deepest sympathies and needing to bring the call to a quick conclusion. 'It's such an awful thing to have happened. Please accept my heartfelt condolences. Well, then, I shall look forward to seeing you at one o'clock tomorrow. Goodbye now.'

Taihei was left standing there holding the receiver, but he didn't have the courage to call back. Instead, he called his daughter.

'Sorry, Dad, a friend's over,' she said, her voice hushed as if worried about being overheard.

'Okay, I'll make it quick. I called that cooking class. What did she mean by shiitake?'

'Oh, right. Tomorrow you're making box sushi. You have to take some salty-sweet shiitake ready simmered in sugar and soy sauce. Um, I think she said about five. Not fresh ones – the dried ones, reconstituted. Sorry, I'll call you back later.'

Shiitake …? The dried ones reconstituted, simmered in sugar and soy sauce …?

Tahei sat down sideways on the chair next to the phone and remained there motionless for a few moments.

Then he made up his mind not to think about shiitake or the cooking class. He went to his study and ran his eyes over the business book he was reading, but the words remained elusive and refused to sink in. Even so, he carried on, glaring defiantly at the text for a couple of hours. Finally, he gave up and went to the kitchen.

I don't want to have to look for any shiitake, let alone cook the damn things! Taihei grumbled to himself as he rooted around. *And I refuse to go to the supermarket to get some*. As it happened, they were surprisingly easy to find, almost as if they were submitting to Taihei's muttered imprecations, in a bag right in the front of the drawer of dried foodstuffs.

At first glance the six small dried shiitake looked more like pebbles than anything you could eat. Taihei stared at them for a moment, then for some reason took out a kitchen knife and brought the blade down on one of them.

'Ow!'

He threw the knife down and frantically sucked on his left index finger, now spurting blood, and stamped his feet. The offending shiitake flew off the chopping board, bounced off the edge of the counter, and landed in the sink with a dispirited clunk. Taihei glared at it reproachfully, then went to get the first aid box. Why the heck had he tried to cut the damn thing in the first place, he wondered as he applied a Band-Aid to his still-bleeding finger.

Box sushi, his daughter had said. As far as Taihei knew, the shiitake used in box sushi was thinly sliced and sprinkled on top of its bed of rice. That's why he'd thought he needed to slice it. But he had to admit it had been a mistake to think of doing so while it was still hard. Once the shiitake had been boiled to soften it up, slicing it should be a simple task for a grown man.

Taihei inwardly cursed the remaining five shiitake sitting there in a row on the counter, and tossed the one that had caused him to hurt his finger into the trash box in the corner of the sink.

He placed them in a pan – the one that Misako had used for making miso soup – and added some sugar and soy sauce. Salty-sweet, was what his daughter had said, and the cooking school woman had said the same when he called. As long as he simmered them with sugar and soy sauce, he couldn't go wrong, surely. Soy sauce was salty, sugar was sweet. Anyone knew that. Well, whatever ... He put the pan on the stove and lit the flame.

The shiitake were hard and it would take time until they were soft, so he sat on the kitchen stool and picked up a dog-eared old notebook that had been left lying on the shelf alongside the row of cookbooks. The cloth cover was the colour of azuki beans and slightly frayed at the corners. It looked like his wife had used it as a recipe book, diary and general notebook. It was the first inkling he had that she'd ever kept something like that. He opened it up at random and read:

When I was a child, I read a story called 'The Soup of the Soup'. The protagonist was a Turk called Hodja, famed for his wit and tall stories. One day he treated a friend to a feast of roast rabbit, but word got around and the next day a friend of that friend dropped by. Hodja treated him to a soup made from the leftovers of the rabbit, but that soup was so tasty that the next day a friend of his friend's friend came to visit. Hodja put a drop of the remains of the soup from the bottom of the pan into a bowl and filled it up with hot water, and fed it to the friend of a friend of a friend, telling him it was the 'soup of the soup'. After that nobody else came to visit. That's basically the sum of the story.

Sometimes I feel like serving up the soup of the soup. I feel like telling someone they shouldn't feel entitled to eat my food. Then again, I've heard that Turkish people take care of their friends and have the custom of inviting visitors to dine with them, so I wonder whether this story shouldn't be read completely differently. For example, perhaps it's saying that you should always serve up something, however modest it may be.

Today my husband brought someone home with him again. He's proud of my cooking. And I am quite a cook. But what comes of him being proud of that?

At lunchtime I used up some leftovers from the refrigerator to make a vegetable jabchae. Jabchae is a Korean dish, vegetables stir-fried with cellophane noodles. A touch of pork really adds to the flavour. Today I used bamboo shoots, yellow chives, shiitake, carrots, bean sprouts and cabbage. Each time the ingredients are different. The only thing I surreptitiously bought especially for this dish was the yellow chives. Yellow chives are expensive, like coriander and straw mushrooms. They're not the sort of thing a housewife would usually put in a lunch she makes for herself, but sometimes you just have to treat yourself. And yellow chives make stir-fry tasty, and look pretty too.

All the vegetables need to be cut to about
the same dimensions as the bean sprouts. The
thin-sliced pork should be seasoned with salt
and sake and fried first. Then you warm some
chopped garlic over a low heat to release the
flavour, before turning the heat up to full and
adding the seasonings one at a time to the pan
and flash frying. Once the meat changes colour,
there's no time to lose. You toss in the shiitake,
carrots, bean sprouts, cabbage, bamboo shoots
and yellow chives, then add the cellophane
noodles reconstituted in hot water – of course
you have to cut them to the right size, otherwise
they'll be unmanageable – and splash with
water, and flavour with Chinese soup stock and
yuzu-flavoured sauce – the type you use for winter
hotpots. Of course you can sweeten it with sugar
or mirin, but I prefer the flavour to be a little
tart, the same way I like adding a little vinegar
to yakisoba or fried rice vermicelli, and I found
it to be surprisingly simple and tasty like this.
But I don't know if everyone in the family will
like it, so I never serve it like this when we're all
together.

My favourite time is when I cook for myself, the
way I please. Cooking for my family is a bit of a
chore, to tell the truth. And it's even worse when
my husband brings home work colleagues, because
I'm so nervous I can't enjoy it at all. Although

you'd have thought that after thirty years or so I
should have got used to it by—

Taihei looked up in alarm – not because of what he'd
read, but because of the smell of burning soy sauce and
sugar assailing his nose.

'Goddamn!'

He hurriedly turned off the gas and opened the lid to
see the chocolatey-looking soy sauce bubbling fiercely,
and the dried shiitake converted into small black stones.
He picked out one to test it, but hastily dropped it back
in with a loud 'Ouch!' Now he had the red trace of a
light burn on his right index finger to match the cut on
the left one.

Frowning, Taihei waited patiently for the black lumps
in the pan to cool. Then he took one out and tested it
between his front teeth. It made an unpleasant crunchy
sound. What was supposed to be a salty-sweet simmered
shiitake tasted bitter, overly salty and a little charred.
On top of that, the blackened lumps were lacking in any
tenderness.

'Hmmmph,' he said dismissively, to no one in particular.

In any case, he hadn't the slightest intention of going
to that stupid cooking class tomorrow – let alone taking
any simmered shiitake with him. What man in his sixties
would get excited about a cooking class anyway?

He added some water to the burned pan, then took
his wife's recipe notebook with him back to his study,
and settled down to read it instead of his usual business
paper. It was filled with gripes, recipes and things she

was proud of. In among comments such as 'My husband can be so sneaky!' or 'I shouldn't have told Sato. I feel so bad about that', she had jotted down recipes or stuck in clippings culled from newspapers and magazines. As he read through them, Taihei recalled various things that he had eaten.

If she disliked cooking so much, she should have told him! The passage he'd read first kept niggling tortuously at the back of his mind. If she didn't like him bringing his coworkers home, he needn't have brought them! But then, although she'd written that having to feed people was such a nuisance, she'd also boasted, 'Mrs Murata said this was so tasty that she wanted the recipe, so I e-mailed it to her,' so he wasn't quite sure what she really felt about it.

Turning the pages, a passage titled 'Shiitake' caught his eye and his hand paused.

The botanical name for shiitake is *Lentinula edodes*, and because 'edodes' sounds like 'Edo desu' ('This is Edo') some people have said it's from the Japanese, but actually it comes from the Greek *εδωδιμος* meaning 'edible'.

I find those rounded Greek letters charming, somehow. I particularly like those two o's with a tail making them look like tadpoles. But more than tadpoles, they look like mushrooms – upside-down mushrooms. And the fact that there are two of them side by side is really cute. It wouldn't be so appealing if there was only one of them.

Maybe I liked them so much because of a story I read when I was little. It was called 'Little Miss Mushroom', about a little girl called Mushroom who gets lost in the forest and meets another mushroom who looks just like herself.

Little Miss Mushroom had short brown hair with red ribbons in it, but I'm convinced she was a shiitake. Two shiitake together are really cute. If I could go back in time to another age, I think I'd choose to go back to the time when I was a shiitake.

Taihei couldn't get his head around the idea that there had been a time when his own wife had been a shiitake. He simply didn't have the imagination. It was like thinking that he'd once been a dog, or a cat, or that he'd been Kobo Daishi or an archbishop of Rome in a previous life.

Feeling peckish, he went back to the kitchen for some 'just add hot water' noodles. They were basically instant chicken ramen, to which you added hot water, closed the lid and waited three minutes before eating just like any others, but were apparently from a famous restaurant, with 'Authentic XX Restaurant Taste!' written in exquisite calligraphy on the packet.

'I thought you might not feel so miserable eating these ones,' his daughter had told him. 'After all, I can't come and cook for you every day.'

Now that he'd filled his stomach with the warm soup, he decided to have a bath and go to bed. With nothing in particular to do, he might as well get an early night.

When he opened his eyes the next morning, he noticed a rather appetising smell.

It was just as if his wife had been stewing something. Well, not his wife, but maybe his daughter had come to make something for him? Spurred by some vague kind of hope or dreamy notion, Taihei left the bedroom and followed his nose.

Sitting atop the gas range in the kitchen was the saucepan as he'd left it the day before, and in it five round black objects floated in a burned brown liquid. He picked one of them out with his fingers. Surprisingly, it had completely transformed since yesterday and was now soft. *The dried ones reconstituted, simmered …* his daughter's words resurfaced in the back of his mind. 'So you guys have reconstituted after all!' he muttered.

His mistake yesterday had been to overlook the step of rehydrating them. Dried goods were made fit for eating by first soaking them in liquid and then simmering them. His ham-fisted measure of putting water into the soy-sauce- and sugar-burned pan and leaving it overnight had unexpectedly resulted in the stonelike lumps swelling into their original mushroom shape. What's more, they were giving off a highly appetising fragrance.

Taihei couldn't resist the temptation to nibble at the edge of the shiitake. While still retaining some crunch, it had absorbed the salty-sweet sauce and was soft and juicy. On top of that, the original flavour of the shiitake seeped through as he bit into it, and it was no exaggeration to say that it tasted exquisite.

Taihei stared at the pan. Then he quickly took out the rest of the mushrooms, removed the stalks and thinly sliced them. Though they had stubbornly repelled his knife yesterday, they now cut surprisingly easily. The liquid left in the pan was slightly salty-sweet, and it occurred to him that he could reduce it to make a thicker sauce. Feeling encouraged, he put everything back into the pan and put the heat on low, careful not to burn it. An initial slightly bitter smell gradually diminished as the flavours of the shiitake stock and seasonings deepened, and a delicious aroma filled the kitchen.

When the simmering shiitake took on an attractive sheen, Taihei decided to go to the class after all. The shiitake were so beautifully prepared that he wanted to show them off. What's more, he hadn't had anything decent to eat since the meal at his wife's funeral. Plus box sushi was one of his favourites.

He checked the address for Tomiko Sugiyama's Cooking School and left the house.

THE SCHOOL WAS IN A SMART residential area in Yoyogi Uehara.

He went up the narrow street and pressed the doorbell of the elegant house on the hill, to be greeted by a small woman who showed him into a large, sparkling-clean kitchen. He sat on a folding chair, holding the Tupperware container of his shiitake, as he waited for Tomiko Sugiyama to appear.

The countertop held an array of small dishes and plates containing carrots, chopped eel, broccolini, bright pink dried fish crumbs, and crushed sesame, along with some clams, eggs, sugar, salt and vinegar. Some clean dishcloths, cooking chopsticks, wooden spatulas and so forth were also neatly laid out.

'Sorry to keep you waiting.' Mrs Tomiko Sugiyama had long hair swept up and secured with a large hairpin, her plump body encased in a dress with a tiny flower-print pattern and covered in a crisp white apron. 'It's a private lesson today.' She smiled at Taihei, who regarded her nervously. So the two of them would be alone together in the kitchen. 'Did you bring the shiitake?'

Her voice rang in his ears. *Shiitake…!* Taihei suddenly felt shy about giving them to her, but seeing him vacillate, she smiled broadly and held out her hand to take the Tupperware he timidly proffered.

'I always get my students to make one thing to bring with them. After all, the good thing about box sushi is that it mixes up a lot of different flavours. You have to prepare all the different ingredients one by one before you can put them all together. It's not as if you can simmer dried gourd, shiitake and carrots all together. You have to prepare them all separately to draw out their individual flavours. Then you arrange them on the vinegared rice. The vinegar does a wonderful job of enhancing their individual characters. The more intense the flavours, the more appealing the final dish. That's why, rather than using only ingredients you yourself have prepared, it's more interesting to get other people to make something too. It adds to the charm of box sushi. Oh my, these shiitake are wonderful,' she said as she opened the lid of the Tupperware container. 'It looks like today's sushi is going to be good.'

She proceeded to wash the rice and put it into the rice cooker along with a strip of dried konbu for flavour, then put some vinegar with sugar and salt on the stove to make the sushi vinegar. As she did so she lectured him on the quantities and how to adjust the heat, but he wasn't taking anything in. He simply responded mechanically to her instructions to take this or pass that.

'When cooking clams,' she said, placing two large shellfish in a pan and splashing some sake over them, 'first you steam them in sake like this, then you take them out and add some soy sauce, sugar and mirin to the juices in the pan and boil it down to make a salty-sweet sauce. It needs to steep overnight, so I have one here that I prepared earlier. Next let's make the thin strips of egg.'

They worked together in silence, beating the eggs, adding a little sugar and a pinch of salt, and pouring the mix into a hot frying pan to make a paper-thin omelette. Taihei stood at Mrs Sugiyama's side, trying to copy her movements as he fried the egg, then nervously turned the paper-thin circle of egg with the tips of his cooking chopsticks. As he cut the finished omelette into thin strips, her gaze fell critically on the plaster on his left index finger and, when he told her what had happened, she laughed.

Once the steamed rice had plumped out nicely, they set to making it ready for the sushi. Mrs Sugiyama put some rice into a wooden tub and added the vinegar mix, stirring it in with the wooden spatula, while it was Taihei's role to stand at her side and cool the rice with a large round fan. Then she added some chopped gourd and carrots, and minced eel. She finely diced half of Taihei's shiitake and added them too, telling him, 'I'll use the other half for the topping.'

'My wife was supposed to come today,' Taihei suddenly said as he fanned the rice.

'Yes, my receptionist told me. Didn't she pass away?' Mrs Sugiyama answered without pausing her hand.

'It was a stroke. It was very – how can I put it? Sudden.'

'How old was she?'

'She's five years younger than me, so fifty-five.'

'That's terrible. Please accept my condolences.'

'It seems that my wife was once a shiitake.'

Taihei himself was taken aback by the words that slipped out of his own mouth without any warning. He had no idea why he should have said such a thing. It was what he had read last night in his wife's recipe book. *If I could go back in time to another age, I think I'd choose to go back to the time when I was a shiitake.* He hadn't thought anything of it when he'd read this, but it now struck him as bizarre. Had his late wife been going strange in the head, by any chance?

'Anyone can be one,' Mrs Sugiyama said equably as she mixed some ingredients in with the vinegared rice.

'Anyone?' Taihei stopped fanning the rice and looked up.

'That's what cooking is all about,' she said. Then she smiled brightly and announced, 'Okay, it's time to dish up,' and cheerfully produced two vermillion-lacquered boxes. She divided the sushi rice, slightly coloured by the salty-sweet stock, between them and pressed it down so that it filled all the corners.

'People don't really understand the art of cooking. Especially people who don't cook. I'm sure your wife must have been a good cook.'

She came to stand next to Taihei as they finished up the dish. It was just a matter of arranging the various ready-prepared ingredients as they pleased, but she said, 'We start with this,' taking some of the fine strips of omelette and fluffing them up as she spread them evenly over the rice. Following her example, Taihei too inlaid his box with the golden egg.

'For example, right now I'm thinking about the time this egg was in the mother hen's belly. By the way, this is a fertilised egg. It was laid at the foot of Mount Daisen. When you hold an egg in your hand, its memories are communicated to you through its shell, you know.'

'Memories?'

'Yes, memories of when I was in the belly of a hen at Mount Daisen come back to me.'

'What?'

'In that sense, my most beautiful memory has to be of the time I was a watershield blossom.'

'A watershield blossom?'

Mrs Sugiyama took each of the ingredients on the dining table in turn and placed them on top of the egg strips.

'I was still just a young girl.' She narrowed her eyes and raised her chin as if remembering the distant past. Her hands paused briefly in their work of arranging the dish as she began talking of the time when she was a watershield bud, swaying all day long, bathed in abundant fresh water and sunlight.

'The marsh was some distance from the village. In winter it was covered with a thin coat of ice, but the spring thaw brought warmer water and in our naturally sunny spot we would feel the life force welling up within us. Our broad leaves were already drifting over the surface of the lake by the time that, feeling the urge to give a big yawn, I stretched up high enough to see two oak trees stretching themselves on the other side of the marsh. The marsh water is so clear that in the sunlight it makes a detailed reflection of the sky, like a mirror. The blue sky and white clouds are reflected between our leaves, and so when the breeze blows we sway together with the sky, bathed in sunlight. As the warm days continue we are unable to contain ourselves any longer and eventually, in early summer, we too produce small flowers. These are rather plain compared to the likes of the water lilies, but the exquisite charm of our buds swelling and proudly bursting open is unforgettable. When the flowering season is over, although we'll eventually send forth new shoots we now begin to slowly disintegrate. You know, the sensation when we are born shuddering in the limpid water, protected by that innocuous but strong, gelatinous mucus, is ... Well, I might be lacking the discretion expected of someone my age, but I'd say it was something

34

close to ecstasy. Spending the days just swaying, swaying, on the surface of the water. That was the happiest time of my life.'

As she talked, Mrs Sugiyama's hands moved between the little dishes and the lacquer box, adding touches of colour to the sushi. 'You should arrange all the ingredients the way you like them.' She sprinkled on some of the pink fish crumbs, then added some pickled lotus root and shiitake. 'It isn't as if there are any rules or fixed ways to do it.'

Taihei nodded and, picking up the small dishes, clumsily added a steamed clam and some broccolini.

'Why, how pretty that is!' Mrs Sugiyama sighed with satisfaction as she contemplated the finished result. It seemed the cooking class was over.

Taihei was given the lacquer box with the sushi that he himself had arranged to take home with him. 'Will we meet again?' he asked before leaving.

Mrs Sugiyama paused a moment then said, 'My cooking classes are oversubscribed, so I ask people who have already participated to refrain from booking another one. Cooking is always a uniquely precious experience, you see. However,' she paused a moment, then added, 'it is possible that sometime, somewhere we will meet again.' She waved goodbye with a big smile.

THAT DAY TAIHEI ate his box sushi, washed down with sake. Somehow it tasted exquisite. Since he had nothing else to do, he took out two more of his wife's notebooks from the shelf of cookbooks in the corner of the kitchen.

There were three in all. They weren't that old – the oldest appeared to be from about ten years ago. Perhaps she had started keeping them from around the time their daughter had left home, leaving the two of them on their own together.

Right from the beginning she had jotted down recipes, gripes and things that interested her. There were things he had eaten and things he hadn't, but he felt particularly interested in those that he hadn't eaten. This was because he intuited that these revealed a side of his wife he had never known. He had the feeling that rising up before him now was the wife he wished he'd known when she was still alive, but who he would never now come to know; the side of her that she herself had wanted to keep secret.

The next day, Taihei started spending time in the kitchen. He decided to try making all of the recipes his wife had written down, one by one. Some were delicious, others less appealing. Sometimes, when he found the flavour to be lacking, he added this or that seasoning and noted it down in his wife's notebook. He would never even consider cooking anything now without these old dog-eared notebooks.

Seven years went by all too quickly, although looking back it was also long enough for a number of things to have happened. Tomiko Sugiyama's Cooking School continued to prosper, her name being regularly bandied around in TV programmes and magazine articles. Taihei's daughter, Sato, married the man who, all those years ago, had often stayed over at her apartment; she later gave birth to a daughter, Ito. However, two years ago she divorced and now she and Ito were living in their own apartment in the city. Ito would be four this year.

Being divorced with a small child, his daughter was naturally lonely – either that, or despite herself she needed his help, for she often called to ask him to come over. She would bring Ito to visit him surprisingly often, too. Taihei did all kinds of things for his granddaughter that his wife would have done had she been alive. Fortunately he could cook, so he could be of some use.

The doorbell rang and Taihei opened the door to see Sato standing there with Ito in tow. 'Grandpa!' his granddaughter shouted, running to him.

It was early March, the Sunday before the Doll Festival, and they had come for lunch. Whether she really meant it or said it only to flatter him, Sato declared, 'Grandpa's box sushi is the best ever!' and begged him to make it for them every year. As they sat down to the lacquered boxes arranged on the table, his daughter and granddaughter would squeal with delight.

As Ito picked up some of the thin strips of egg in her little fingers, Taihei would ask her, 'What's that?'

'*Omwet.*'

'And that?'

'Shiitako.'

She hadn't learned how to pronounce 'omelette' and 'shiitake' properly yet, even though she was getting quite big.

For his part, having been cooking for some time now, Taihei had begun to have some understanding of the art of cooking. Now he, too, could remember the time when he'd been a shiitake. He could see himself sitting quietly on an old chestnut oak log feeling the breeze on his cheeks.

And he recalled that he hadn't been alone, for snuggled up next to him, trembling slightly, there had been another shiitake.

The Life Story of a
Sewing Machine

IT WAS SUMMER WHEN THE SEWING MACHINE appeared in the window of the antique shop on the high street. It was still there in autumn, when the leaves of the gingko trees lining the street turned yellow and the nuts spread their rancid smell of butyric acid. Even when the leaves had all withered and fallen and been cleaned away, it was still there.

Yuka gazed at the sewing machine on her way to and from work. It had a bit of damage here and there, but the black head with its soft lines atop the neatly varnished stand, the letters *SINGER* in gold amidst an ornamental design, possibly flowers, in green, red and yellow paint, and even the beautiful shape of the decorative iron legs extending below the stand, were a joy to behold.

She stopped so often to look at it that one day the elderly shopkeeper came out to talk to her.

'This one was made in America, in 1923. It's a Singer Model 66. It's very rare to find one with these colours – especially the red.' He pointed at the red almond-shaped motifs either side of the lettering. 'It's called a Red Eye.

See, those look a bit like eyes, don't they? I was really lucky to get my hands on something like this. I just happened to find it at an estate sale in a town in rural America.'

'Estate sale?'

'That's when someone dies, and their home and all its furnishings are sold off. You can sometimes get hold of old crockery, ornaments and whatnot surprisingly cheaply. If the owner had good taste and looked after them, you can get quality items in good condition.'

Yuka looked at the sewing machine again. Of course it must have been used by someone, but still the thought came as something of a shock.

'If you like it, I'll give you a good price,' the shopkeeper said with a genial smile.

'It's lovely, but I haven't got anywhere to put it,' Yuka told him honestly, and laughed good-naturedly.

'Are you after a sewing machine?' he asked.

Yuka realised that she had never even thought about whether she wanted a sewing machine.

'It's not that I particularly want one, no.'

'So, it's just for decoration? Like an ornament? If that's the case…' he said, waving her into the shop. Apparently he had plenty of time on his hands.

He wasn't being pushy, Yuka thought. He'd just invited her in because he had nothing better to do. The shop's interior was a hodgepodge of second-hand items, from glass lampshades, hibachi braziers, and wall clocks, to personal seals, Imari dishes, bellows cameras and phonographs. They were worn but well-dusted, and items that needed polishing were well-polished.

As she went in, the shopkeeper lit a kerosene heater at the centre of the store. It had a cylindrical grey body, with decorative holes in it like lacework, through which you could see the amber flame flickering into life.

'Is this old too?'

Somehow she had the feeling the shopkeeper was proud of it and was hoping she would ask this, so she did.

'It was manufactured, oh, around the same time as that sewing machine in the window. 1920s, I'd say. It's American, made by the Perfection Stove Company. The cylinder is steel, except for this glass bit here where you can see the flame. They're pretty popular. Have a look over here,' he said, leading her to a table with antique teacups on it, along with salt and pepper pots, ashtrays and cutlery.

'This here is actually a sewing machine stand. It's made of oak,' he said, rapping his knuckles on it. 'And look at those legs! People nowadays don't have any use for heavy sewing machines, but they like this design. Lots of people remove the machine head, and use the stand alone like this as a decorative piece of furniture. You can put it in the corner of your living room and use it as a coffee table, and some youngsters even use them as a dining table. It looks good with some books on it. You can use these as bookends, too,' he added, picking up an old solid metal iron. 'Although that's maybe a bit too over the top.'

The sewing machine-stand-turned-table and irons-turned-bookends had gained a new lease of life with a decorative use unrelated to their original purpose.

'If you want an antique sewing machine but don't have much space,' the shopkeeper went on briskly, as though he didn't want her to leave, 'then there's always this sort of thing.'

He gently stroked a semicylindrical wooden lid with a handle on the top. He undid a hook on the side, and a sewing machine with gold decorations on its black head emerged. This one too carried the name *SINGER*.

'Singer,' Yuka read out loud without realising it.

'There are a lot of them around, that's for sure. It's the world's biggest maker, after all. It set the standard for sewing machines.'

The shopkeeper looked proud as though he himself had created it, and then stroked his prominent stubble-covered chin.

'Still, this is a Singer VS3 model. It's even older than the one in the window, and was made in England around the end of the nineteenth century. The design of branch and leaves together with a badge was Victorian, apparently.'

Stroking the gold design fondly, he added, 'You know, every sewing machine has its own life story.'

Yuka ignored this, and moved further into the shop. She'd never been in here before, yet somehow all the objects aroused in her a feeling of nostalgia, and she didn't feel like she was seeing them for the first time.

Eventually she reached the far end, where there were some boxes piled up, possibly containing objects waiting to be unpacked, but what caught her eye was yet another sewing machine tossed carelessly on top of them.

'Is this one a Singer too?'

'Which one?'

The shopkeeper pushed his way through the cramped shop to see what she was looking at

'Oh, that one. No, it isn't a Singer,' he said, a troubled look on his face. 'In this state, you can't really tell what it is, though.' He laughed.

'You can't?'

'Well, it's been painted over, so you can't see the original design and colour. The hand crank was added later, too, so goodness only knows what make it is. But I think it's probably from the Japanese maker Pine, now the Janome Sewing Machine Company – one of the Model 100-30 treadle machines they made in the late 1920s.'

'But this one isn't a treadle machine.'

'Right. In this state you can't really know what it is.' He smiled.

'Is it for sale?' Yuka touched its damaged body gently.

'Suppose it is, are you going to buy it?'

It wasn't by any stretch of the imagination an attractive object that could be used as an ornament. It'd be more appropriate to say it really was junk, a relatively bulky object and waste of space that nobody would buy even as a joke.

'Why is it here?'

'Some young people whose work it is to clear out properties of the dead brought it here.'

'Properties of the dead?'

'That's right. People leave stuff behind when they die.'

Yuka turned and looked around the shop again. Of course, the owners of all these antiques were probably already dead.

She looked at the sewing machine again. 'Does it work?'

'No, it doesn't.'

'I thought not.'

'But then, its parts are in much better condition than you would think to look at it. At least, it had been well looked after, and you'd have thought it would work. But you see, it doesn't have a heart.'

'A heart?'

Yuka looked at him, but he didn't seem to be teasing her. The old man seemed lost in thought for a while, until finally he answered her.

'That's right. That's why it doesn't work.'

—

THE PINE MODEL 100-30 was born and raised in Koganei village in Tokyo's Kitatama district, but no sooner was it given the stamp of approval to go out into the world than it was packed off to the dressmaking school in the factory grounds.

At that time, Koganei was known for being a remote area in the pristine upper reaches of the Tamagawa canal where it flows though the oak and birch forests of Musashino. However, being such a conveniently large area, it was probably inevitable that it would be chosen for a large development. The land was cleared, and the factory and school built. The employees also started building small houses along the hastily constructed railway. Those were boom times.

Some of the other sewing machines born at the same time went to work in good households, but it wasn't unusual to be sent to a dressmaking school. Back then, sewing was the only work considered appropriate for women, and dressmaking schools were springing up all over the country. Some of the girls were attending because they needed to find employment, while others were well-to-do young ladies undergoing domestic training to prepare them for marriage.

You should have seen how the eyes of all the young women seated in rows in the classroom shone with energy and ambition as they learned how to thread the machine and work the pedal, manage the seam allowance and handle different fabrics!

'Ladies! Your resolution this year – to make lots of money working and buy plenty of whatever you like!' proclaimed the Imperial Sewing Machine Company's massive advertising campaign in 1936.

'Modern woman can make a good living for herself if push comes to shove!'

'Turn your dressmaking and handicraft hobbies into cash!'

Needless to say, these rapid-fire catchphrases lit bright flames in the hearts of women who longed to enjoy to the full the livelihood that was spreading from the city centre out to the residential suburbs. All that was needed was to have a machine at home for your exclusive use, a large sewing machine that you had free access to. Surely that wasn't too much to ask? If you put this big machine before a man, he wouldn't know what to do with it. Only mothers and daughters would be able to operate this iron device. If you just had one of those in your home, the space it took up, just half a tatami mat, would be exclusively women's terrain.

Strangely enough, it was the war that was behind women's unadulterated ambition to become manufacturers-cum-consumers. As the continent went up in flames, women embraced the slogan 'To my husband the gun, to me the sewing machine'.

Thus women learned that, for those on the home front supporting the war, sewing machines were a weapon for frugality and production, and service to the nation.

Their hearts were further struck by the catchphrase 'Pedal and produce to buy bonds!' – a parody of the wartime slogan for population policy 'Give birth! Reproduce for your country!' At the time everyone was being encouraged to buy government bonds, but to be honest it wasn't clear how much of the sewing machine earnings went into savings. In reality, many of the women attending dressmaking schools were war widows or had become the head of the family during the absence of their husbands, and for them it was necessary to make clothes for their children and take in piecework they could do at home.

In any case, not only did the country promote frugality, but there was demand for uniforms and backpacks for soldiers, and women flocked to dressmaking schools to learn needlework skills.

THE BIGGEST SCANDAL at Koganei happened before the war situation had become too severe, and concerned a party dress that a student of the dressmaking school was sewing for her graduation project.

The sewing machines were in orderly rows in the classroom, and each was allocated a number, but naturally there were some that did especially neat seams, some whose needles glided easily through the cloth to produce smooth stitching, and others that were difficult to handle. Number 17 was the sewing machine that everyone wanted to use. The teacher decided who got to use which machine, and there was a subtle but cut-throat fight between the girls to get in the teacher's good books in the hope of being allowed to use it.

Regularly on number 17 at the time was Miss Itokawa, the mild-mannered, beautiful daughter of a merchant. A fair-complexioned girl, she was efficient, careful in her work and loved by everyone, but one day she ran into misfortune. It happened when she was on the very final stretch of her graduation project, and about to add decorative white tulle to the collar, sleeves and hem of her dress.

A sewing machine has no will of its own or control over what anyone does, so there was nothing it could do to prevent it.

The evening before that fateful day, one girl snuck back into the dimly lit classroom after all the other pupils had gone home. According to the calendar it was spring, but it was still March and chilly.

Concealing her face beneath the woollen stole she wore over her arrow-feather-patterned kimono, she looked furtively around to check nobody was there, then made a beeline for sewing machine number 17, pulled out the head that had been neatly stowed away, took off the throat plate and removed the bobbin case from the shuttle hook. Then she casually replaced the throat plate, put the stolen bobbin case in the sleeve of her kimono, and left the classroom covering her face with her kimono sleeves – probably to conceal the smile that broke out on her face despite herself rather than out of any need to hide. She glided out of the classroom on tiptoes.

The next day, when it was time for class, Miss Itokawa sat down as always at sewing machine number 17. She stood the head up, took some thread from the drawer, and set it up. But when she removed the throat plate to take the bobbin case out, she realised something was wrong, and paled. Uneasily, she opened the sewing machine's drawer and rummaged around inside it with her white fingers, her eyebrows slightly furrowed.

'Is something wrong?' the girl next to her asked, and Miss Itokawa flushed and bit her lip. Then the teacher arrived, and as always they rose to their feet and bowed.

'So, everyone, today we shall put the finishing touches to our graduation projects,' she said.

At that moment, Miss Itokawa abruptly threw herself down over the sewing machine table and began softly weeping. Her classmates and the teacher all started asking her what the matter was.

As for what happened next, why did it occur precisely at that moment? Was it deliberate? Or was it evidence that you couldn't conceal such a deed? Either way, there was a soft clang from a seat behind her, and everyone turned to see the girl, who last night had secretly taken the bobbin case out, sitting with her mouth agape, looking pale. The bobbin case bounced awkwardly on the wooden floor and rolled unsteadily into the corner. Everyone followed it with their gaze in silence.

Sensing the tense atmosphere, Miss Itokawa raised her head and turned to look behind her.

What she did next stunned everyone. Until that moment she had been head down in tears, but now she stood up and, without even bothering to wipe her damp and reddened cheeks, ran resolutely to the desk at the back, raised her arm high in the air and swiped it down.

There was a loud smack, and the thief held her hands to her cheek. But the normally mild-mannered, gentle Miss Itokawa was not content with just having slapped her classmate. She ran back to sewing machine number 17, opened the drawer and took out some dressmaking scissors, then went back and picked up her classmate's dress for the graduation project from the sewing machine table, and laid into it with the scissors.

Screams pierced the classroom, the teacher shrieked, and the school caretaker ran to call the headmaster.

In the end, the thief's graduation dress was stitched back together by Miss Itokawa and sewing machine number 17, and looked amazingly good with its unique slash design. Miss Itokawa added the lovely tulle to the collar, cuffs and hem of her own dress, but she apparently did so at home, not in the classroom. She and the thief had been secretly exchanging letters, and it later became clear from their close friendship that the bobbin case scandal had been the result of a lovers' tiff. In the end, though, it never was known what exactly had led to the theft of the bobbin case or why it had been such a big scandal. That was not something that the 100-30, sewing machine number 17, could possibly know about.

However, at the school's graduation party, while the students wearing the party dresses they had made clustered around the 100-30 machine on display chattering away together, Miss Itokawa and the other girl held hands and gazed at each other loath to part, as though they wished that moment would last for eternity.

And for a long time after that, the white party frocks made for the graduation project were the most beautiful dresses the 100-30 had ever made.

In the era that followed, the only work it produced was dull, as it was a time when beauty was irrelevant and functionality was everything.

SOMETIME LATER, the 100-30 was sold off to the Japan Women's Association's work centre in Takinogawa, closer to central Tokyo.

This was a place where war widows or women who had lost everything in the air raids could learn dressmaking for free. It was similar to the Koganei dressmaking school in the sense that women went there to gain dressmaking skills. Needless to say, however, at the work centre in Takinogawa they were not making party dresses adorned with tulle frills.

While the work centre was a school, it was also a mass production factory so there was never any thought for sewing pretty clothes or making nice designs: they were making purely functional trousers and jackets for civilian and military uniforms, knapsacks, caps and so forth – their daily work was to sew for all they were worth and produce the ordered items by the specified date.

The women doing the work were all dressed in baggy work pants, and while the military police inspector was on patrol their lips were firmly closed and they focused on working the sewing machine pedal.

The only sound in the work centre, other than the voice of the teacher explaining what to do, was the rhythmical kerclunk, kerclunk of the sewing machines, with the occasional snap as a needle stopped and thread was cut, or the rubbing of the cloth.

The women at the work centre were extremely serious, so there was never any extravagance like the dressmaking school's graduation party dresses, and they would use their lunch breaks to cuddle their children in the work centre's day nursery. Some young mothers would even suckle their babies whether or not they were hungry for milk.

Upon finishing the three months of training many of them would start taking in piecework at home, but even if they had work it was not easy to get hold of a sewing machine. Fewer machines were being produced, and most new ones were sent to munitions factories. It was fine for those who already had a sewing machine as part of their bridal trousseau, but it was another matter for those whose houses had burned down in air raids and had escaped with just the clothes on their back. Those women were able to borrow a machine in the work centre, and they worked from eight thirty in the morning to four thirty in the afternoon doing mountains of sewing in the service of the country.

One of these, a widow by the name of Kame Yoshida, finally managed to get her hands on her very own 100-30 sewing machine.

Owing to the many factories located in Takinogawa, the area was frequently the target of air raids and those who survived these were being urged to evacuate. With few people left there the danger was even greater, and eventually the order came to demolish the work centre and put its sewing machines to use in munitions factories or loan them out to skilled seamstresses. And so the sewing machines were scattered here and there, and the 100-30 ended up with Kame.

Kame lived in Akabane with her elderly mother-in-law who had dementia, and her two young boys not yet in primary school. Her husband was at the front and, with the old woman and children to support, she had to feed the family somehow. In addition to the subcontracted work from munitions factories, she would take in whatever sewing she could, such as mending for the neighbourhood association. She worked the sewing machine hard from morning to night, and was really good at stitching together anything, from her children's old nappies to scraps of cloth to make dishcloths and floor cushions. Her persistence was extraordinary, as she frantically saved every single scrap of cloth, no matter how worn or small, and would make them all into something. Nothing was wasted.

Things mount up, as the saying goes, and she even used scraps the size of her big toe to make a mattress. She made split-toe socks, and used old stockings to make socks for children, and the interfacing from old obi sashes to make baggy work pants. For the 100-30, it was a far cry from the old days when it made pure silk white dresses. And given how Kame pushed it so hard and was so extremely penny-pinching, the needle grew ever blunter, yet still Kame paid no heed to the fact that the holes in the fabric were growing rougher by the day. By the spring of 1945, there was not a shred of pride left in the 100-30 for having once been number 17.

And then that fateful day came.

It was before dawn on the fourteenth of April. At around nine o'clock the previous night a warning had been issued, and Kame evacuated to the air raid shelter with her grumbling mother-in-law and two children. Had she taken the trouble to cover the 100-30 with even just one water-soaked mattress, it might have been saved from such a cruel fate. In any case, Kame never did come back to rescue it, so she herself must either have died in the air raid or been injured and taken away. Either way, the sewing machine never saw her again.

There was a loud bang and moments later incendiary bombs came raining down. The 100-30 was stowed away in a corner of the narrow, west-facing corridor of Kame's small rented house. An incendiary bomb set fire to some rags that she had been saving and they went up in flames. Unfortunately a scrap she had left pinned by the sewing machine needle was hanging down, and the flames from the pile of rags underneath, fanned by a breeze, started licking its edges.

The iron legs were hardly affected by such weak flames, but once the flames reached the wooden stand it could no longer remain unscathed. It was forced to endure being burned to a cinder, yet still the head could possibly have been saved had it stopped there. Unfortunately for the 100-30, though, the house next door was also on fire and as the flames spread to Kame's house the whole place soon became engulfed. Then the firestorm came and the 100-30 was suddenly blasted away in the hot wind.

For the sewing machine, with a dignified bearing and fated to be stationary, the shock all but caused it to lose its reason for existence. The 100-30, warped by the flames and with its needle broken, was embedded in the ground. It was unlikely a sewing machine could survive such a calamity.

At last the fire burned itself out. The wooden parts of the 100-30 had been mostly reduced to ashes. It would obviously never see Kame again, but of more pressing concern was the fact that it was so mangled it could hardly even be called a sewing machine any more. The

100-30 lay on its side half buried in the ground, its head bent backwards. Never before had it been in such a state! Lying idle in the ashen streets reduced to embers, smoke rising up all around it, it could only be mistaken for part of the rubble.

The 100-30 remained in this odd posture for several days. The quality of the iron was such that it would never rust away, and its fate was surely to remain as part of the natural landscape, like a stone or rock formation. However, it was not to be. Once again it was caught up in a shocking episode.

It was early morning. A man was out walking, dragging one leg. He appeared to be scavenging in the burned-out ruins, and was throwing relatively unscathed cans into a basket on his back, mumbling and grumbling to himself. The moment he caught sight of the 100-30 buried in the rubble, his eyes lit up. Then, what should he take from the basket on his back but an axe, which he brought down on the sewing machine with all his might.

Had the 100-30 been given the power to cry out, no doubt it would have done so for all it was worth. But, of course, machines weren't afforded that sort of function, so the evil deed was carried out entirely in silence.

Having stolen the 100-30's head, or rather its carcass, the man set off running through the burned-out ruins holding it in his grubby hands without even bothering to put it in his basket. Having lost its beautiful wooden stand, the splendid legs reminiscent of Western art, and the pedal that you could say was the life force of a treadle sewing machine, you might assume that it would be taken away and thrown into a furnace, melted down in the inferno to red molten iron and turned into some weapon or other to end up overseas – the usual fate of a lump of iron in wartime.

Yet strangely enough, this is not what happened.

The man took several trains, eventually arriving at a farmhouse in the countryside intending to exchange the 100-30 for some beans and potatoes and the like. Unfortunately, though, it wasn't worth as much as he had estimated he could get for it in good condition. The 100-30 was heavy, and damaged. Not only was the needle broken, the throat plate and shuttle hook were also missing. The bobbin winder spring was broken, and sand and soot had got inside its works. In other words it needed repairing, but nobody there was capable of doing this.

Having been wrong about being able to get a good price for the 100-30, the man treated it mercilessly. His home was a rather flimsy affair, with little space for a sewing machine. And so, late at night, when everyone was asleep, he took a shovel and dug a gaping hole under the eaves. It appeared he intended to hide the unfortunate sewing machine there. Even considering its lamentable state, this was an exceptionally dark place for it to end up in.

The man picked it up and tossed it into the hole. Then he must have felt a bit guilty after all, for he pulled it out again, wiped off the mud with a hand towel and went off to look for something. He returned with some old newspapers, wrapped the 100-30 up in them, and once again dropped it into the hole. Then he shovelled earth in on top.

And so it was that the 100-30 came to be buried alive.

SOME TIME PASSED before the 100-30 saw the light of day again, when a different man dug it up.

There is no way of knowing who he was, or how he was connected to the previous man. However, given what happened next, we can deduce that the 100-30 was taken to a bustling black market where it was displayed alongside all manner of junk.

The war was over in the world in which the 100-30 reappeared. Everyone was saying things that they would never have said during wartime. There were more men around, demobilised soldiers wearing gaiters and with three-day stubble, and street urchins who moved as nimbly as animals. Women who had worn their hair in severe buns in wartime now wore it loose or in pretty plaits. All jostled in the suffocating and cramped space of the market, as American Occupation jeeps roared up and down the roads.

'Hey, I'll take that,' a woman said, pointing at the 100-30. She was wearing an ill-fitting jacket, no doubt a LARA charity handout, over well-worn baggy work pants, but still she managed to be quite stylish with loosely waved shoulder-length hair and a touch of lipstick.

After haggling fiercely, she grudgingly pulled out some bank notes from her pocket and handed them over. In return she had the man take the heavy sewing machine back to her house in a two-wheeled cart.

The woman lived in Yanaka, an area in central Tokyo that had escaped damage in the air raids, and was densely packed with cramped, wooden terraced houses. She was a widow, but lived with two men in the tiny room beyond the dirt-floor kitchen. During the day she took in work sticking together paper bags, and at night she waited at table in a restaurant run by an acquaintance. She attended the classes for widows at the Compatriots Aid Society-sponsored dressmaking school, having heard that there was work for those who completed the course. If only she had not sold her sewing machine during the war, she would have better work.

One of the men she lived with worked as an art director for a tableau vivant in Shinjuku, while the other was a demobilised soldier with nothing resembling a proper job. The woman ordered this man to repair the sewing machine.

'Look, you said you did engineering at university, didn't you? Fix this up so I can use it.'

It was all very well for her to say this, but how on earth was he supposed to do it? Once he heard that the household income would dramatically increase if she could use it, however, he put his mind to it. That afternoon he left the house, and came home with an old sewing machine manual and a book about sewing machines in a foreign language that he had picked up somewhere, and sat there with his arms folded reading them for a while. Then he suddenly got up and went out again, returning later with what appeared to be a few bits of junk but were actually sewing machine parts.

Finally the man got down to work on the 100-30. First, he carefully unscrewed the blackened remains of the stand from which the sewing machine had been so pitifully hacked away with the axe. Then, paying no heed to the woman's objections, he dismantled the head. It was covered in dirt from having been treated so roughly, and the man now carefully wiped it clean with a rag. Then he used some bicycle lubricating oil and sandpaper to remove the rust from all the individual parts, and some wood to reinforce the spool pin and part of the broken throat plate. Next, he neatly filed the shuttle hook, bobbin and bobbin case, which were the wrong type for the machine, to make them fit.

Then he put the 100-30 together again. He made a wooden stand to keep it steady, placed it on top, and screwed it down. He attached a handle like on an ice-shaving machine to the circular hand wheel on the right side of the head to make the needle bar go up and down. The black paint was flaking off the body here and there, but the newly attached handle was silvery green.

For the first time in many years, needle thread was placed on the spool pin and wound onto the bobbin inside the shuttle hook. The man took the hand towel hanging from his waist, raised the presser foot and inserted the towel. Then he quietly lowered the presser foot and fixed it in place, exhaled, and turned the handle. There was an unpleasant kerthump, and the needle came to an abrupt halt. He searched for what was wrong and, continually referring to the foreign-language book, dismantled it once more and reassembled it. He repeated this numerous times.

And so, the 100-30 was brought back to life.

Meanwhile the woman had started attending the dressmaking school for widows. She had learned a little already as a girl, and she had always liked clothes, so she made good progress. When the 100-30 was miraculously reborn as a hand crank sewing machine, she hadn't yet finished her course but nevertheless she immediately went out around the neighbourhood taking orders. And that meant she could leave her job in the restaurant, which she didn't like very much.

After so many years, the 100-30 once again stitched a skirt. It was a far cry from the beautiful seams of the number 17 machine that girls had once competed to use, but it stitched whatever was ordered of it in rough and earnest straight lines: skirts, dresses, shirts, children's clothes, trousers, men's suits, and even winter overcoats. It patched the bottoms and knees of children's clothes, and attached new collars and cuffs to worn-out men's shirts. It also stitched taffeta, twill, satin, velvet, wool and synthetic fibres. And leather. And beautiful colours, and patterned fabrics.

Little by little, the woman's lifestyle became more affluent. She did her hair and made beautiful clothes for herself. Of the two men she lived with, she was currently having relations with the artistic director. At first she had slept with the demobilised soldier too, but he was taciturn and boring, and she ended up falling in love with the other man. Eventually she left, taking the artistic director and the 100-30 with her.

Just once, the demobilised soldier turned up at the woman's apartment near Shinjuku. He took a chisel from his tool belt and threatened her with it, ordering her to come home. She refused, and he stormed into the apartment without even taking off his shoes. Catching sight of the 100-30 on a reading desk in the corner, he ran to it, stooped down, and caught hold of the head.

'Hey, what do you think you're doing?' the woman shrieked, her face pale with anger.

'I'm the one who made it usable again. I'm going to take it with me.'

'What do you mean? If you take it, I won't be able to work, will I?'

'Not my problem. I know this machine inside out.'

'Stop it. There's no need to be so nasty just because I jilted you.'

She edged her way over to the reading desk and, with the 100-30 between them, they began to tussle with one another. The next moment, the woman grasped the stand and the man the head, and they each started trying to pull it from the other.

'Let go!'

'You let go!'

'Look, you're short of money, aren't you? How much do you want?'

'It's not a matter of money, stupid!'

The pair were pulling with all their might when suddenly the man looked at the 100-30 and, appearing to come to his senses, let go. The woman fell onto her back and lay face up with the sewing machine on her stomach, grimacing in pain.

'Ow! That was vicious of you!'

The woman didn't know why the man had let go first, but in any case she put the 100-30 back on the reading desk. After they had recovered their breath, the man once again approached the sewing machine, taking a screwdriver from his tool belt.

'Don't touch it!' the woman screamed.

But the man merely tightened a screw in the stand that had come loose in the struggle, then took the hand towel from his belt, secured it between the needle plate and the foot, and turned the handle to check its condition. Then he fondled the 100-30 much as though he were caressing a woman, picked up his chisel from where it had fallen on the floor, and left.

The main commotion happened after that. It hadn't occurred to the woman in the thick of it all, but after the man left she went pale with fear. In her belly she was carrying a child.

The artistic director returned home to find her groaning and clutching her belly. He went white as a sheet and ran out of the apartment to fetch a doctor. The woman wailed as he roundly cursed the demobilised soldier. Had she suffered a miscarriage at that moment, it was entirely possible that the woman might have flown into a rage and destroyed the 100-30 for having caused the calamity.

However, after listening to her belly with his stethoscope the doctor said, 'I can hear the heartbeat, so look after yourself and see how it goes.' Two or three days later, around the time the bruise on the side of her belly turned yellow, she could feel the baby moving around a lot, so they knew it was growing and well-protected by amniotic fluid.

The 100-30, having been the target of her fury, if anything, now became a symbol of good fortune. The whole story of how the demobilised soldier had marched in red with rage became the topic of conversation at the dinner table for some time thereafter, much exaggerated and embellished. The woman kept up her work on the sewing machine right up until the time she gave birth and was back sitting at the machine right afterwards.

One day the artistic director brought some blue paint home from work and repainted the 100-30. He didn't touch the elaborate machinery, but painted only the safe part of the body a deep blue, and let it dry.

'Why did you do that?' the woman asked.

'This sewing machine belongs to you, not to him,' the artistic director answered, the brush still in his hand.

The money the woman made from her needlework disappeared quickly into the cost of milk for the child and into the birth of their next child. And in between jobs, the woman stitched nappies and clothes for the children. And now that the children were running around the place, their father, now the artistic director of a film studio, made a cover for the sewing machine in his spare time so they couldn't touch it.

By the time the second child had started walking and a third child was on the way, the couple moved home and bought a new sewing machine. The 100-30 was left covered, and was no longer called upon for anything unless it was urgent. Fortunately they had moved to a fairly large council house, and since it had been transformed into a hand-crank sewing machine it didn't occupy much space, so while it was rarely used it was not scrapped. However, it was shut away in a cupboard most of the time.

The next time the 100-30 saw the light of day again was when the eldest child started attending primary school and said that she wanted to make things on the sewing machine just like her mum did.

The woman's new sewing machine had long since been converted to electric, and since a hand-crank sewing machine that stitched slowly would be more appropriate for a small child, the 100-30 was once again pulled out of storage. That day the 100-30, which had once sewn even a man's tuxedo, was operated by the little girl's fingers as she attached a wide ribbon to the edge of a square scrap of seersucker cloth to make an apron. The next day she attached small square patches as pockets.

Next she stitched some triangular cloths to make a bag for drawing paper and crayons, then cushions, then trousers for her teddy bear. And a doll made from felt stuffed with silk cotton.

The 100-30 was the little girl's playmate for several years until she was able to use her mother's electric sewing machine. At some point her mother stopped taking in sewing work, and only occasionally made things to order. People were already buying clothes off the peg by that time. Now the 100-30 was no longer needed, it was again covered and stowed away in the cupboard.

And so more years went by, more even than when it had been buried in the ground. The woman saw her daughters marry and said her last farewell to the artistic director, yet still made no move to take the 100-30 out of the cupboard in the council home where she lived alone.

When it was eventually taken out of the cupboard where it had lain forgotten for so many years, it was by the woman's eldest daughter. Not only was she now grown up, she was already touching upon old age herself and her mother had just died.

When the woman was still alive she had told her daughter, 'When I die, put that old sewing machine in my grave with my ashes, will you? It made it possible for me to raise you. It's like my own arm.

And so the daughter took out the 100-30 intending to do as her mother wished, but the priest at the temple where the artistic director was buried insisted that there was no space to bury such a large item with her.

In the end, the daughter removed the shuttle containing the shuttle hook and the bobbin case and put it into the urn with her mother's ashes.

That's why the 100-30 no longer had a heart.

Global Positioning System

'COS THAT'S THE RULE.' The merry-go-round operator shot Yuki an annoyed look.

She gripped her little sister's tiny mitten-clad hand. The younger girl wore a wool knit cap with flaps that came down over her ears.

Set amid Tokyo's downtown office buildings, the small amusement park near Korakuen subway station was brightly festooned with coloured lights for the holiday season. Businessmen leaving work for the day walked briskly by on their way to the station entrance, ignoring the merry-go-round, which stood silent and unmoving. When the girls approached, the youth whose part-time job it was to operate the ride had been engrossed in a manga comic, an electric heater blazing away at his feet.

'Children three and under must be accompanied by an adult,' he continued officiously. 'Understand? That means a grown-up has to ride too.'

'But she's with *me*,' said Yuki.

'*You're* not an adult. You've got to be at least sixteen. Where's your mum?'

'At work.'

'Your dad?'

'Same.'

'You mean you two are here all alone?'

'Uh-huh.'

'Man, I bet you're going to be in big trouble.'

'Why shouldn't we come here on our own?'

'You can come if you want, but I can't let you on the ride.'

The youth turned back to his comic book.

Yuki glared at him for a while but he studiously ignored her, so she turned to her sister. The little girl clung to the railing, gazing raptly at the colourful horses on their metal poles. Yuki rested her hands on her sister's shoulders and crouched down behind her. 'Don't worry, Rui, I'll figure something out.' The little girl nodded trustingly and turned her attention back to the horses. 'C'mon,' Yuki said, 'let's go find a grown-up.' She took her sister's mitten-clad hands in hers and swivelled her round. The little girl craned her neck, her eyes fixed longingly on the merry-go-round.

'I'm still not letting you on the ride,' muttered the pimply youth, looking up anxiously from his manga. 'Not without a parent. If you get hurt, I'll get blamed,' he said, shaking his head. His breath shot out white into the cold night air.

Ignoring him, Yuki turned and walked away, the little girl trailing after her.

'Where we goin', Yuki?'

'There must be *someone* who'll go on the merry-go-round with us.'

It was more an expression of hope than an answer to Rui's question, but the little girl appeared satisfied.

The girls' parents weren't due home until after nine o'clock. Most evenings, Yuki and Rui went to their grandmother's, a few stations west across the river on the main commuter line. But today she was outside Tokyo attending a friend's wake. 'You two'll have to fend for yourselves tonight,' their mother had informed them that morning before leaving for work.

'Can we go to the playground?'

'Yes. But be sure you're home early enough to do your homework before bedtime,' said her mother. 'And eat a good supper – there's chicken curry in the fridge.'

Yuki knew full well her mother was thinking of the local park, which had a small children's playground.

'Okay, Mum,' she replied, visions of the merry-go-round dancing in her head.

Yuki had been to the merry-go-round at night only once, back when she was in primary school. Rui was just a baby then and in day care until their mother got home from work. One evening, when their father was out of town on business and their grandmother was again off doing something, Yuki had ridden the subway alone to her mother's office downtown as soon as her after-school activities ended. She waited there until her mother finished work and they walked back to Korakuen station together, passing the amusement park all lit up for the holidays. Yuki had been enraptured by its dazzling merry-go-round.

'Well, I guess one ride won't hurt,' relented her mother, uncharacteristically, and together they climbed onto the merry-go-round just as the operator was getting ready to shut it down for the night.

There was hardly anyone else about at that hour, and it felt to Yuki as though they had the merry-go-round all to themselves. They whirled round and round, slowly rising and falling on their horses to an oppressively cheerful melody. Yuki had never forgotten her surprise and joy as the music ended and the ride slowed, only to begin revolving once more as though by magic.

Since then Yuki had begged her mother dozens of times to take her back to the merry-go-round – but to no avail. Her mother refused even to let her come to her office after school. 'You're a fifth-grader now, Yuki,' her mother had explained recently, 'you're old enough to stay home and look after the house. Plus, you'd have to bring Rui with you, and it's not safe for you two to ride the subway alone.'

But last month Yuki had noticed that the newspaper delivery boy had left them some free tickets to the Korakuen amusement park. Her mother had tossed them in the rubbish bin, but Yuki had fished them out and saved them for the next time she and Rui were left at home alone until late at night.

We'll just go and ride the merry-go-round and come straight back, Yuki thought to herself, *that's all...*

And so, desperately gripping Rui's tiny hand, which perpetually seemed on the verge of slipping out of its mitten, Yuki and her little sister had ridden the subway to the amusement park; the carriage had been full of grown-ups, some of whom trod painfully on the girls' toes with their high heels.

She was determined not to go home disappointed.

It was already past seven o'clock and the park's poplar trees, stripped bare for winter, stood out white in the darkness. Yuki watched grown-ups in heavy winter coats hurry by before she spotted an old man standing near the ticket booth.

She tightened her grip on Rui's tiny hand.

ABOUT TWO MONTHS before her husband's birthday, Yoko Higashi had telephoned her three daughters.

Mari and Nana, her two oldest, were both married with children of their own. The most they ever did for their father's birthday was call or send a card or a small present. Yoko was quite sure that, unprompted, they were unlikely to pay a visit this year either. But she had a reason for wanting to bring her three daughters together and an idea how she might manage it.

Her youngest daughter, Fumi, was still single and worked downtown as something called a 'food coordinator'. Despite Fumi's lack of family responsibilities, whenever Yoko asked her to do anything, her daughter always protested she was too busy. Yoko was determined not to leave room for such an excuse this time.

'Hi, Granny.'

The first call Yoko made was to her second daughter, Nana, whom she spoke to the most. But Nana was out and it was her eight-year-old son, Shota, who answered the phone.

'Good evening, Sho-chan.'

'Granny, guess what year it is?'

'Let's see, it's the Year of the Dog, isn't it?'

'It's the twenty-fifth year since Ultraman defeated Margodon and brought peace to Earth!' the boy fairly shouted into the receiver. 'But guess what? Now the monsters are back and Mebius has been sent to Earth to destroy them!'

'Is that so? My, you *are* well informed … By the way, Sho-chan, is your mother at home?'

'No, she's not here … Granny, do you know the name of Mebius' teacher?'

'Möbius? You mean the man who thought up that loop you make by twisting a strip of paper and joining the ends? I'm sure his teacher was someone very smart…'

'I'm talking about Ultraman Mebius, Granny. D'ya know *his* teacher's name?'

'I'm sorry, Sho-chan, your granny's not up on these things … Now, could you—'

'It's Ultraman Taro!'

Yoko could almost see the look of triumph on her grandson's face.

'Is that so? How interesting! Now, Sho-chan, is your father there?'

'Uh-huh.'

'Could I speak to him?'

'Hi there, Mrs H.'

Nana's husband, Kenji, standing beside Shota listening to the entire exchange, immediately took the receiver from his son.

'Sorry 'bout that, Mrs H. We're both totally hooked on that show. It's an awesome homage to Nebula M78!

Takes me back to *my* childhood! Shota and I just got through watching the original *Ultraman* TV series together on DVD. I hadn't seen it for years!'

At the other end of the telephone line, Shota could be overheard pestering his father to let him quiz his grandmother some more. Yoko began to fear she would be trapped in a loop of adolescent science fiction. She cleared her throat loudly.

'Kenji?'

'Yes, Mrs H?'

'Where's Nana?'

'Tonight's her night out with her girlfriends.'

'Well, I'm calling because her father's birthday is coming up fairly soon and I was rather hoping you might all be free to come over for lunch.'

'That's in December, right?'

'Yes, Saturday the ninth.'

'Well, I'll have to check at work – we're always swamped at the end of the year. I might have to go in to the office on the weekends.'

Yoko didn't mind if her son-in-law didn't come – in fact, she rather preferred he didn't.

'That's quite all right, Kenji,' she said with a dismissive wave of the hand, as though he were standing in front of her. 'Don't worry if you can't make it. But what about Nana?'

'Oh, I'm sure she'll be there. She wouldn't miss her old man's birthday party. Anyway, I'll tell her to give you a call as soon as she gets back.'

'Could you do that, please?'

'No problem, Mrs H.'

Yoko always found her son-in-law's manner of speech somewhat juvenile. Kenji Hayashiba, who was two years younger than his wife, was almost the size of a sumo wrestler on account of his job as a product developer for a major snack food brand, which involved sampling test products all day long.

Next, Yoko called her youngest daughter, Fumi. Predictably, Fumi's answering machine picked up. Yoko started to leave a message but was abruptly cut off by a loud beep before she could finish what she wanted to say. She called back. This time she succeeded in telling the machine that she wished to host a birthday party for her husband and hoped her three daughters would be able to attend.

Then, after a moment's reflection, she redialled Fumi's number a third time. As soon as the outgoing message ended, Yoko hurriedly added, 'I think your father wants to talk about money or something,' but before she could think of what to say next the answering machine cut her off one last time.

That left Mari. Yoko had planned to ask the usually reliable Nana to pass her message on to Mari for her, but since Nana was out and still had not returned her call by the time Yoko went to bed that night, she made up her mind to set her alarm clock for five a.m. the next morning. One could never be too careful when telephoning Mari, who lived in a seaside town south of San Francisco where her marine biologist husband had recently taken a job as a visiting researcher.

'Just add seven hours to whatever time it is in Japan,' Mari had instructed her mother, giving her a long telephone number with lots of zeros in front. 'Or subtract seventeen. And remember, we're usually one day behind you.'

This was enough to make Yoko's head spin. Usually, she'd get all in a muddle about how many hours she should be adding or subtracting, and then give up altogether on the idea of calling. Or else she'd *think* she'd calculated correctly only to hear Mari pick up the phone and mumble something like, 'Sorry, Mum, I'm really sleepy ... can't talk now,' and hang up on her.

Mari had said the best time to catch her was 'sometime in the morning'. But since seven a.m. in California was midnight in Japan, that proved virtually impossible for Yoko. So she and her daughter had reached a compromise: Yoko would wake up at five a.m. – noon on the West Coast – and this way she had a pretty good chance of getting hold of her daughter.

But, unfortunately, Mari seemed to be out that day. The phone rang several times and then a voice suddenly started speaking in English. Yoko quickly put down the receiver in a panic. It took about a minute before she realised it had been her daughter's answering machine.

'Don't they understand? I'm over seventy years old!' she railed at no one in particular. She couldn't understand why her forty-something daughters put her through such torture.

She collected herself and dialled Mari's number again.

This time, after listening to something that sounded like 'Pleats-libya-name-in-message, I-gay-bar-chew-assume-ass-posse-beau', she blurted into the receiver, 'I'm having a birthday party for your father. Please ask Nana about it.'

Then, feeling completely exhausted, she went back to bed.

CONSIDERING THEIR MOTHER had gone to the extent of summoning Mari back from California, the three sisters concluded it was no ordinary birthday party.

Initially, Mari – through Nana – had told their mother that during the Christmas holidays she and her husband and their two sons were planning to travel to the East Coast of the United States instead of returning to Japan. Although logistically it might be feasible to return to Tokyo in December, Mari said, finances were tight due to their recent relocation overseas.

Yoko – also through Nana – responded to Mari by saying that since the birthday party didn't coincide with the Christmas holidays she would like her to come on her own, if at all possible.

'I wouldn't have to play this silly telephone game if you two would just talk directly,' complained Nana to her older sister over the phone late one night, a ritual she had got accustomed to of late.

'I've tried calling Mum any number of times but she's never home,' protested Mari, repeating the same excuse Yoko had given Nana.

'Apparently Dad wants to talk about money.'

'What money? I thought they didn't have any assets to speak of apart from the house.'

'Perhaps he's got something stashed away in the stock market,' suggested Nana.

'Even if he did, you think Dad would talk about it?' shot back Mari. 'He's the type who'd rather die than bring up that sort of thing face to face.'

'I dunno. Maybe he would, maybe he wouldn't. Or perhaps Mum just wants us all together because his illness is getting worse.'

'Is it? I was afraid of that. I wonder if he'll recognise me,' Mari fretted.

'Don't worry, he'll remember you as soon as he sees you,' said Nana. 'He's that way with me, anyway.'

'I suppose,' said Mari, 'but this trip is going to blow a hole in our family budget.'

'Still, I think it's best you come. Anyway, you know Mum; she won't back down. She even brought up how the currency markets are in your favour.'

'What on earth does that mean?'

'Well, Shin gets paid in dollars in California, right?' said Nana, referring to Mari's husband. 'So, since the dollar is strong at the moment flights to Japan should be relatively cheap. Anyway, that's what Mum says.'

'Fine, I'll come,' Mari sighed resignedly. She began calculating in her mind how many days she could convince her husband and sons to let her go away for.

Mari landed in Japan two days before her father's birthday. The next day, she found her way to a bookstore café in a trendy new commercial development in central Tokyo to meet her two younger siblings, Nana and Fumi, for lunch.

'Wholefood eateries like this are popping up all over,' observed Nana. 'We have one near us.'

'This isn't just wholefood, it's vegan,' Fumi corrected her. She was quite a few years younger than the other two and the only one still in her thirties.

'Is there a difference?'

'Seriously? They're *completely* different! Wholefood includes meat – this place only serves plants.'

'You mean it's vegetarian?'

'Some vegetarians eat eggs and dairy – dietary vegans don't consume any animal products. Then there are raw-food vegans, paleo vegans, fruitarians and so on – it gets rather complicated, actually – but places like this just call themselves "vegan".'

'I guess we're behind the times, aren't we, Nana?' said Mari, who'd been about to say she knew all about veganism from living in California. But she changed her mind when she saw how cowed Nana looked after Fumi's lecture.

Just then their drinks arrived – steaming mugs of home-made ginger toddy – and the three sisters fell momentarily silent while the waitress set them down on the table.

'I've only been away a short time but it's amazing how much Tokyo has changed,' said Mari, breaking the silence. 'Speaking of which, how's Dad?'

'Good physically, it seems,' said Nana. 'But he's changed in little ways.'

'Such as?'

'He's always ridden his bike everywhere without a problem. Now he keeps getting into accidents.'

'What! He'd better stop before he gets hurt, hadn't he?'

'That's easy for you to say. *He* doesn't think he's putting himself in any danger, so it's hard to make him stop.'

'Well, at least he doesn't drive.'

'It's no laughing matter – he hardly pays any attention to what's going on around him and will suddenly turn left instead of right, that sort of thing. Mum says he keeps running into walls and stuff and has fallen off his bike any number of times.'

'Sounds dangerous.'

'Plus he's started coming home late.'

'Coming home? From where?'

'His haiku and chess clubs, mainly.'

'He still does haiku, then?'

'Every month. He goes on his own, too.'

'By bicycle?'

'Of course not – by train. But he's liable to come home late for no reason.'

'Why does Mum let him go on his own? Someone should go with him!'

'Apparently the doctor says, as long as he's still mobile, Mum shouldn't fuss over him too much.'

'But is he capable of managing on his own?'

'He's fine taking the train and asking for directions if needs be.'

The three women sighed in unison.

Shohei Higashi's illness had manifested itself three summers ago. Around that time, things had started disappearing from the house and their father had grown increasingly forgetful. Then, to cap things off, came the incident with their father's high school reunion, which he'd been attending every other year, in the same place, for decades.

Shohei had dressed, caught the bus to the local commuter rail station and ridden the train to Ochanomizu. Then, forgetting why he was there, he'd got straight back on the train and come home, much to his wife's astonishment. Thinking her husband must have forgotten something, Yoko said something to him about the reunion. Flustered, he rushed out of the house again. This time he made it only as far as the local railway station. When Yoko returned from shopping she found him in the living room staring off into space.

'How was the reunion, dear?'

'Huh? Oh, it was cancelled,' Shohei said before disappearing into his study. Watching him go, Yoko had a sinking feeling something must have happened and rang up one of his classmates' wives. She was told the reunion had taken place as usual.

Yoko suspected Shohei might be suffering from the same awful-sounding affliction as his late older brother years ago (so awful-sounding, in fact, that people now referred to it as 'dementia'). So she spoke to a friend who gave her the address of a local outpatient clinic called the Forgetfulness Centre.

Shohei scored twenty out of thirty on the clinic's mental assessment test. The doctor gave a diagnosis of early-stage Alzheimer's and wrote out a prescription for some pills.

'This won't halt or reverse his condition,' the doctor explained, handing the prescription to Yoko. 'The most we can do is slow its progression by a couple of years. The results vary from person to person.'

The doctor's words reminded Yoko of the good fairy in *Sleeping Beauty* who informs the king and queen she cannot undo the curse the evil witch has placed on their daughter; the most she can do is to weaken it, so instead of dying when she pricks her finger on the spindle the girl will merely fall into a one-hundred-year sleep.

'It's been three years already,' observed Fumi, raising the mug of warm toddy to her mouth, now that it had cooled down a bit. The implication, unspoken but understood by all three, was that Shohei had reached the point where it was possible, according to the doctor, that the efficacy of his medication could begin to wear off and his condition take a turn for the worse.

They began to debate what to buy their father as a gift for his birthday, which was their purpose in meeting up that day. Various ideas were raised – a scarf, a pair of gloves, a hot-water bottle, a novel about a chess player – but in the end they settled on a pair of 'senior-friendly' mobile phones, which a young man in a Santa Claus suit was loudly hawking outside the nearby train station. Done up in bright red and green wrapping paper, with white ribbons, the two boxes seemed the perfect gift for a pair of old lovebirds.

ON THE NINTH OF DECEMBER, just past noon, the three sisters arrived at the small two-storey house in the suburbs of Tokyo where their parents, Shohei and Yoko Higashi, lived.

One by one, Fumi opened the Tupperware boxes full of the food she had prepared. There were three varieties of rice balls in different colours – pink flaked salmon, green mustard leaves, and yellow scrambled egg – fried chicken chunks lightly flavoured with curry powder, creamy sweet-and-sour potato salad with raisins and red and yellow roasted bell peppers in a Japanese-style fish-broth marinade. With the exception of the marinated bell peppers – which the four women polished off by themselves, exclaiming, 'What a perfect party dish!' 'You *must* give me the recipe!' and 'Who would've thought bell peppers went so well with Japanese food?' – the menu had clearly been designed more with Fumi's eight-year-old nephew in mind than her elderly father, whose birthday they had gathered to celebrate.

For his part, Shohei concentrated his attention on the fried chicken and rice balls with mustard leaves.

'Try this, Dad, it's really good,' Fumi said, heaping some potato salad onto his plate. Shohei immediately set about painstakingly picking out the raisins one by one using his chopsticks. This drew muted protests from Yoko and Nana, primarily on account of the bad example they feared it was setting Shohei's impressionable grandson. But Shohei ignored them and continued hunting for the tiny, shrivelled-up offending objects like a man on a mission. Shota, meanwhile, was oblivious to what was going on around him, intent as he was on stuffing himself with as much of everything as he could before rushing off to the next room to watch the *Ultraman Taro* DVD he'd rented from the video shop outside the station.

In the train on the way there, Nana had told her only son the adults had important things they needed to discuss and he could watch TV as soon as he finished eating. At this, Shota wrinkled his brow and said the grown-ups could do as they pleased but that he refused to watch anything except *Ultraman Taro*, as he'd planned to stay home and do in the first place.

'A fat lot of good it is saying that *now*,' said his mother, her anger rising. 'You're the one who decided to come when you found out Aunt Fumi was doing the cooking. If you were going to be like this, young man, you should have brought that stupid DVD with you!'

But the eight-year-old hadn't even batted an eyelid. 'There *is* a video shop near Granny's house where we can rent it, you know,' he replied, not without reason.

Thus Shota had succeeded in having his cake and eating it too. Once he had finished his aunt's specially prepared lunch, he was packed off as promised to the next room to watch his beloved *Ultraman Taro*, with one of the mini pear tarts Fumi had picked up on the way for dessert, and a square of Ghirardelli chocolate his Aunt Mari had brought back from California.

Once the adults were alone, the four women began thinking of broaching the matter that was on all their minds. But before they knew it the conversation had ground to a halt, as one by one their attention was drawn to something Shohei was doing with his fingers.

Having finished eating his own pear tart, Shohei, still seated at the table, was engrossed in carefully smoothing out the piece of aluminium foil it had been sitting on. In the process, some of the filling left on the foil got onto his finger and he gave a start; he quickly licked it off and carefully wiped his finger with a tissue. Then he turned his attention back to the foil. When he was done smoothing out all the fine creases, he slipped the foil under his dessert plate for safe keeping and looked around the table at the four women. Seeing that each had an identical piece of foil on her plate, he demanded that they pass these to him too, and he proceeded to smooth them out one at a time.

'This kind of thing has become a favourite pastime of your father's lately,' said Yoko somewhat sheepishly in response to the questioning looks on her daughters' faces as they watched him.

'You mean, like handicrafts or something?' asked Fumi.

'Yes, handicrafts, or rather…'

'Playing with foil?'

It was Mari who spoke.

'Erm, yes, foil and … other things.'

After the tarts were all gone Shohei, too, had been given one of Mari's Ghirardelli chocolates. The now empty wrapper lay on the table in front of him. It consisted of a single piece of foil, silver on the inside and coloured on the outside with the manufacturer's name and logo, folded over and sealed along two opposite edges. Shohei had watched somewhat disapprovingly as Mari carelessly tore open the chocolate wrapper for him, prising it apart at one of the edges. After popping the chocolate square uninterestedly into his mouth, Shohei immediately turned his attention to the wrapper and avidly began to smooth it out against the tabletop with his fingers, as he'd done with the pieces of foil, as though willing it to revert to its original form.

'Dad?'

'Huh?'

Shohei looked up.

'What do you plan to do with those, Dad?'

'What, these? I'll keep them, of course. Never know when they might come in handy,' Shohei replied gravely.

'Keep them where? Under the plate like that other one?'

'Of course not. That's just, you know, temporary. I've got a much safer place for them ... Yoko, do you mind?'

Shohei's tone was firm and betrayed no hint of any mental infirmity.

'Certainly, dear,' said Yoko, getting up.

Their father's manner reminded his three daughters of how, back in the days when he was still working, first as a middle-school principal and later as head of the local public library, he would ask their mother to fetch his lacquered writing box whenever he had important business to attend to. They braced themselves, fully expecting that now, finally, the conversation would turn from foil wrappers to the subject of their inheritance.

But instead of their father's familiar old writing box – with its inkstone, ink stick, brush and carved stone seal

– their mother returned to the room with a beat-up-looking biscuit tin. Taking it from Yoko, Shohei hesitated for a moment, his fingers poised uncertainly on the edges; at last he wrenched off the lid, promptly sending a shower of carefully stacked sweet wrappers flying across the table, which still bore the remains of the birthday feast, and down onto the carpet.

The three sisters looked on dumbstruck, barely daring to breathe, as the squares of multicoloured foil fluttered slowly to the floor. Shohei got down on his knees, an expression of disgust on his face, and began gathering them up and smoothing out the wrinkles one sheet at a time. As soon as his daughters had recovered from their initial shock, they joined in and began to gather up the rest of the wrappers, saying, 'It's okay, Dad, we'll make them all nice again,' and 'We'll put them all back in the box for you.'

But even after the wrappers were back in the box and the tea had grown cold, still the subject of the sisters' inheritance did not come up. Slowly it began to dawn on them that from the very beginning their father had never intended to have such a conversation.

'But *you* said you weren't coming home for New Year,' said Yoko when Mari gently reproached her. 'So much can change in just a year.' Her eldest daughter retorted that in that case she should have just explained the situation and told her to come home anyway. 'Well, your father *did* say once that he wanted to discuss money matters sometime when you were all together,' Yoko claimed dubiously in her defence.

While her mother and older sibling were quibbling, Fumi took a fresh look at her surroundings. The living room had changed quite a bit since her last visit, which was admittedly some time ago. It appeared her father's hoarding habit was not limited to sweet wrappers and foil. On the sideboard, instead of the bottles of foreign vodka, whisky and the like which Fumi remembered from her childhood, she now counted a collection of some fifteen or so empty jars of Shiseido MG5 men's pomade, while on the bookshelf, lined up against the spines of Shohei's books, was an impressive array of empty Frontier cigarette packs.

'At any rate, your father refuses to throw anything away,' Yoko said sharply, clearly annoyed at having to keep making excuses for everything.

'Is *that* a symptom of his illness too?' asked Mari.

Yoko merely shrugged.

Another factor contributing to the room's somewhat odd atmosphere, Fumi noticed, was that stuck to the walls, where Shohei's favourite paintings had once hung, there was now an eclectic assortment of yellowing old diplomas, certificates, and awards.

'What's up with these, Mum?' asked Yoko's youngest and most stylish daughter, wrinkling her brow.

'Your father enjoys looking at them.'

'No way! You don't really, Dad, do you?' snickered Fumi, turning to her father. Only then did she realise her mistake.

Beaming, Shohei pointed to a faded piece of paper pinned to the wall that read: *1992 Neighbourhood Chess*

Championship, 4th Place – Shohei Higashi. 'Look, that's my name!' he exclaimed proudly. 'I won that!'

'Wow, fourth place!', 'You're amazing, Dad!' Shohei's two older daughters cooed sycophantically. Fumi continued frowning.

Seeing the sudden improvement in her husband's mood, Yoko decided to strike while the iron was hot.

'See, dear. Didn't I tell you? Everyone thinks you're wonderful. You've accomplished so much!'

'Have I?'

'Of course, dear. You were the head of the library.'

'Was I?'

'Yes. That's why your daughters are all here today.'

'Is it? Are they?'

'Yes, dear.'

Watching as their parents launched into what felt like an inept impression of a two-man comedy routine, even Mari and Nana began to look more than a little uncomfortable.

'So is *this* why you wanted us to come today, Mum?' hissed Fumi in a cross between a question and a reproach. 'Couldn't you have spared us the charade?'

'How else could I get you to come?' Yoko shot back, her voice hardening again.

'I *do* come for New Year,' Fumi protested.

'But Mari's away in America this New Year – *and* next!'

'So now it's *my* fault, is it?'

'And even for New Year,' continued Yoko, ignoring Mari's comment, 'you come one day, Fumi, and Nana comes a different day – we never have you both here together.'

'That may be, but aren't you embarrassed to have guests over, what with "Neighbourhood Chess Championship, 4th Place" and whatnot stuck all over the walls? How can I bring Tomoki here?'

'So what's more important – your father or your boyfriend?'

'You really want me to answer that?'

'Anyway, what's wrong with putting up those old prizes, if it makes your father happy?'

'Huh? What are you all talking about? What makes me happy?'

'Your chess prize, dear.'

'Chess prize? Where? Oh, is that mine? Look, my name!' exclaimed Shohei with newfound delight. 'I won that!'

Yoko stood up triumphantly and went off to the kitchen to make more tea.

Mari, eager to change the mood, exclaimed in an exaggerated way, as though suddenly remembering something, 'Oh, how silly of me! I almost forgot! This is for you, Dad.'

She reached into her bag and took out a small box with a white ribbon on it, then handed it to her father.

'Huh? What's this?'

'Open it.'

'Here, lemme unwrap it first, Dad, then you can do the rest,' interrupted Nana, grabbing it out of his hands. 'If you start messing with this wrapping paper we'll be here for hours!'

Shohei gazed at the paper covetously as Nana unwrapped the present.

Just then Yoko returned to the living room.

'My, what's this? A birthday present?' she said as she poured fresh tea into their cups.

'Yes – you get one too, Mum.'

'Do I?'

'It's from all three of us.'

Fumi rolled her eyes and looked away. Her older sisters had talked her into putting the phone contracts under her name. True, they had both agreed to give her ten thousand yen at the end of the following year. But as the total cost of the two plans came to just over three thousand yen per month, or thirty-six thousand per year, Fumi was being forced to bear an unequal burden. Plus, she'd be on the hook for any extra charges if her parents exceeded their monthly calling limit. Of course, her sisters reasoned that Fumi earned more than they did *and* was still single. But in her sisters' eyes none of this seemed to alter the fact that the present was from all three of them.

'They're equipped with GPS.'

'G–P–S?' queried Yoko.

'Short for "Global Positioning System" – it uses satellites to track your location, just like a car navigation system.'

'In other words, you'll be able to tell where Dad is when he goes out.'

'Really? It can do *that*?'

Yoko tossed aside the empty tea tray she was still holding and grabbed the mobile phone. Adjusting her reading glasses on her nose, she tilted her chin up slightly and peered down at the small device.

'Wait a sec, Mum. We'll get it set up for you. Here, let me have Dad's, too.'

While Nana fiddled with Yoko's shiny new pink-coloured phone, and Mari her father's grey one, Fumi gazed at Shohei's fourth-place prize from the neighbourhood chess association. Global Positioning System – it was a grand-sounding name, wasn't it? Fumi imagined a host of gleaming satellites hurtling through outer space, tracking one's every movement, even to the very ends of the Earth. Never mind that these days her father rarely ventured out of his immediate neighbourhood.

As these thoughts passed through Fumi's mind, her mother and two older sisters prattled on in the background...

'Now, make sure you take it with you when you go out, got it? Okay, let's practice – answer the phone when it rings. There, it's ringing. Now, touch the green flashing spot on the screen. No, green...the flashing circle – that's right! Now talk...in a normal voice – you don't have to shout. Hello? See, it works! There, you did it! That wasn't so hard, was it?'

Fumi cringed inwardly at their fawning, coaxing tones, as though they were speaking to a very young, dimwitted child. Finally, unable to stand it any longer, she went to the kitchen and took a beer from the fridge. Popping it open, she walked down the hallway to the bottom of the stairs and sat down on the second step.

From the TV room on the other side of the wall came the sounds of a superhuman being from outer space battling to save the Earth from monsters.

THE FIRST REAL TEST of the GPS-equipped mobile phones that Shohei and Yoko Higashi had received from their three daughters came one weekday evening just before Christmas, after Mari had returned to California.

'Nana, your father is missing!' Nana was busy getting dinner ready when her mother rang up in a panic. 'He went out to his haiku club this morning and hasn't come home yet,' she continued. 'It seems he got there all right, so he must have lost his way coming home. I've tried calling the community centre and the library, thinking he might have stopped in there, but no one's seen him!'

'Now, calm down, Mum – this is exactly why we got you those mobiles ... Have you checked it to see where he is?'

'Oh...'

Yoko was momentarily at a loss for words. She glanced around for her pink phone before realising she was talking to her daughter on it.

Nana told her to call back on the land line, then walked her through the process of locating Shohei using the GPS function, while she did the same on her own mobile.

'It says, "No signal"! What does *that* mean?' asked Yoko indignantly. 'I thought you said it could track him any place on Earth!'

He must be underground or somewhere the signal can't reach.'

'I'll try again ... still no signal. What's wrong with this thing? It's useless!'

'You can't give up after just one or two tries, Mum, you – *ahhhhh*!'

Yoko thought her eardrum would burst. 'What is it? What are you screaming about?'

'The fish! The fish is burning! Sorry, Mum, I've got to go – I'll call you back after I finish making dinner.'

Yoko hung up and again began going through the procedure Nana had shown her for tracking Shohei's GPS signal on her mobile phone. A spinning wheel appeared on the screen, then a map unfolded from the centre of it. On it was a red flashing dot. It was her husband!

Just then the telephone rang. Yoko frantically picked up the receiver.

'Is that you, dear?'

'No, Mum, it's Nana. Everything's under control here for now. Anyway, I just checked my phone again – Dad appears to be wandering around Shinjuku.'

'That's not far – I'll go over there right away.'

'Hold on a sec ... He's on the move again!'

'Huh? Oh dear, oh dear, what*ever* is your father up to?'

'Did you try calling?'

'You mean him? Dozens of times! He won't answer. His phone must be in the pocket of his coat where he can't hear it. Oh, this is terrible! What are we going to do?'

'Okay, he's moved again. Now he's near me, at Meidaimae.'

'What? I thought you said he was in Shinjuku!'

'The train, Mum. He's on the Keio line.'

'Why would he take the Keio?'

'Now he's at Chitose-Karasuyama…'

'Oh, no. He must have gotten on a commuter express. I better go fetch him—'

'Fetch him? Mum, how're you going to do that? He's on a moving train!'

'I'll call the train company and get them to ask the conductor to look for an old man riding the train…'

'Now he's at Chofu.'

'So *that's* where he was heading!'

'What do you mean?'

'When your father and I were first married we lived in an apartment in Minami-Asagaya, and our landlord at the time had a daughter who was an acupuncturist in Chofu. Well, that time when your father hurt his back he went to Chofu to see her.'

'And is that some kind of special memory or something?'

'No, not particularly. But it's probably the only time he's been on the Keio line—'

'He's coming back, Mum! It says he's at Tsutsujigaoka now.'

'Ah, so he is. Good for him! He's trying to get back on his own!'

'He simply got on the wrong train – it could happen to anyone.'

'Hurray! He did it! Once he gets back to Shinjuku he can change to the Chuo line. Or maybe he'll get a taxi home. Oh, what a relief! This GPS is a lifesaver!'

But Yoko's sense of relief proved fleeting, for no sooner had Shohei reached Shinjuku than the signal from his mobile phone went dead again, causing mother and daughter to pass an anxious and uneasy forty minutes or so.

After giving Shota his supper, Nana rang up Fumi to let her know what was happening. Now, in addition to Yoko and Nana, the youngest Higashi daughter was glued to her mobile phone.

Fretting that her father must have unwittingly switched off his mobile, or else that the battery had died, Nana called her mother back to say she thought they had best notify the police. But she had barely got out the words when Yoko cried out, 'Look, the red dot has come on again!'

'Really? Where? Oh, there it is, at Korakuen. I see – he must have got on the Marunouchi subway line at Shinjuku. That's why we couldn't see him.'

'I'll call the station and ask them to pick him up. I wonder what number I should dial.'

'Hold on. He's still moving.'

'Not again!'

Slowly, the red dot began drifting away from Korakuen subway station. Then, after going a short distance, it stopped. It seemed Shohei Higashi had had enough of riding trains for a while.

LEADING HER LITTLE SISTER by the hand, Yuki approached the old man in front of the ticket booth.

'Good evening,' Yuki said.

'Good evening,' Rui parroted.

'Good evening,' replied Shohei.

'We want to ride the merry-go-round but they won't let us on without a grown-up. Will you ride it with us? I have tickets.'

Shohei didn't know why he was there. He couldn't remember why he had left home or how to get back. All he knew was he had spotted the Ferris wheel from the station and walked towards it, like a moth drawn to a flame. And now he was standing talking to these two little girls.

'But what about your, you know? he began. 'I mean, where is your, erm…?'

'Our mum?'

'That's it. Your mother.'

'She's working late tonight. But she said we could come here and ride the merry-go-round. Just once – then we'll go straight home. But they won't let us ride it without a grown-up.'

'But what about your – you know, the other one? Don't you have a, erm…?'

'Our dad?'

'That's it. Your father.'

'He's at work too. My sister and I have to be home before they get back. We just want to ride the merry-go-round once, then we'll leave. Please ride with us.'

'But do you know how to – I mean, do you know where your what-you-just-said is?'

'Our home? Don't worry. We came here on our own – we can get back alright.'

'Are you sure?'

'Don't worry, we'll be okay, thank you. Now will you come on the merry-go-round with us?'

Shohei nodded and took the small hand proffered to him.

'You're back, huh?' muttered the merry-go-round operator, eyeing them dubiously.

'We brought our grandpa,' said Yuki.

'That's right, I'm their grandpa,' the old man confirmed.

The youth shrugged and opened the gate for them.

Under the lights of the Christmas illuminations, Yuki's and Rui's faces shone with delight. Yuki climbed onto a horse and Shohei took the one next to hers.

'The little one's got to ride with you, gramps,' said the operator, giving Rui a heave up and placing her on the back of Shohei's horse, in between his legs.

'I'll run it twice – don't get down until it comes to a complete stop the second time.'

The music began to play and the merry-go-round started moving, the horses rising and falling on their poles. Shohei gave an audible gasp and with one hand held firmly onto the tiny girl the young man had placed in his lap. The merry-go-round spun round and round, scattering rays of light into the darkness. From time to time, the girl on the other horse turned and smiled and waved at him with her free hand. The small, warm body pressed heavily against Shohei's thighs and stomach, stirring long-forgotten but somehow very familiar memories. The little girl in his lap gave a gleeful, piercing laugh and turned her head and looked up at him.

All Shohei knew – as the melody whose name he had forgotten played and the carousel sped round – was that what he had to do at this moment was hold on, for all he was worth, to the tiny life that had been entrusted to him. He began to hum the notes of the familiar melody, *la-la-la-la, la-la-la-la, la-la-la-la-la,* and an emotion he was tempted to call happiness welled up inside him.

For the umpteenth time that day, Shohei's GPS-enabled mobile phone vibrated away forgotten and unnoticed in the pocket of his coat, where he had put it that morning, as he and two little girls raced round and round on their horses.

Kirara's Paper Plane

THAT DAY, AS ALWAYS, Kenta made his appearance without warning.

Then again, who could he have told he was coming? And how? *Okay, ready or not, here I come!* No, he couldn't – and anyway there was no one to tell.

After his death, Kenta had initially been unaware he'd become a ghost. He would search out his old friends and run over, calling out to them. But he was invisible, apparently, even when standing right in front of them. Shouting didn't help either – he was inaudible, too, it turned out, and it only made him more dejected.

Yet it was not as though Kenta himself ever had any prior warning he was about to appear. No one came and said, *Well, Kenta, today's the day!* or *Kenta, my boy, it's time you were off!* Even after all this time, he was no closer to understanding *why* it happened. First off, he was unaware he existed until the moment he actually made his appearance. And then he didn't know where he'd been before that or what he'd been doing. If there was a world beyond this one, an afterlife, then there was no continuity between the Kenta of this world and the Kenta of that one. His self which had existed in this world, before he died, had been a living thing; his self which reappeared from time to time after he passed over to the other side was a ghost – he'd grasped this distinction. Beyond that, he knew nothing.

In the beginning Kenta's appearances had been fairly frequent. Lately, however, it seemed to him they had grown less so. It was the dramatic changes in the cityscape that made him realise how long he'd been away. And while in the past his visits had been long, now they were not only less frequent but they never lasted more than about a day. Nor was there any discernible pattern to them – he did not return on his death anniversary, or for the Obon Festival, or even every year for that matter. It occurred to Kenta that after the memory of his existence had faded completely from the minds of those who had known him, his appearances, too, might cease altogether. But one thing he understood very clearly: it was his fate to relive his death at the end of each visit. While Kenta didn't dislike the visits themselves all that much, when the moment came for him to be hit by a car in the street near Ueno Station, he was seized by an acute sense of dread.

And so once again Kenta suddenly found himself in the station's pedestrian underpass. It was his usual place. Above ground the scenery changed in the blink of an eye but the underpass always looked exactly as he'd known it. Of course, the vagrants and urchins that had congregated there in those postwar days had long since vanished. Gone, too, were the awful stench and the gangsters, the pimps, the prostitutes and the perverts

– at least in the form they had existed back then. Still, there was no other place to which Kenta could lay claim, and so the underpass was where he always appeared. But there was no point hanging around there on his own, so straightaway he went up the steps and outside onto the street. Hardly anyone was about, for it was still early morning and the trains had not yet started running.

With a great flapping of wings, a flock of crows flew down and settled in some trees on the edge of the park across the street. Kenta's pangs of hunger returned. He could not imagine what it was like *not* to feel hungry. To him, privation and this world were synonymous.

He set off with unsteady steps, his stomach growling in protest. The odour of food scraps left out in bins overnight drifted through the streets. As though mesmerised by the smell, Kenta's feet carried him to a street lined with bars and restaurants. In one doorway hung a half-length red curtain with the word *ramen* on it. As he walked past he heard light-hearted chatter.

At that moment the door slid open and – with an exuberant 'Good night!' – a group of young women spilled into the street. Their heavily made-up faces stirred a distant memory. *Whores*, thought Kenta. A delicious meaty, fatty aroma mingled with soy sauce wafted into the street as a rather hunched old woman followed the young women out, took down the red curtain and went back inside. Having seen off her last customers, she was closing up for the day.

The gaggle of women broke into twos and threes and piled into taxis.

One of the women remained behind and started off up the street. Kenta followed her with his eyes. She turned a corner and disappeared; he raced after her. Pausing at the corner, Kenta scanned the street. Spotting her again, he began to follow her. Her shoulder-length, dyed-brown hair hung down in large curls and she wore a sequinned denim skirt and short white jacket with ballet flats instead of high heels. Kenta had no particular reason for following her other than a vague sense that she resembled someone he'd once known.

This was how he typically spent his days when he returned to this world.

AT THE TOP OF THE SLOPE the woman turned into a narrow side street, barely more than an alleyway. After casting a cautious look about, she approached a small two-storey block of flats, with three doors on each floor facing onto an open corridor and an iron staircase leading up. She climbed the stairs to the second floor, stopped at the middle door and slipped something through the letter box. Then she turned and pattered quickly down the stairs and hurried back up the alley towards the main street.

From behind a telephone pole Kenta watched the woman go. He was about to follow her when he heard a sound and looked up. The door of the flat which the woman had stopped in front of opened and a little girl stepped out, sleepily rubbing her eyes. She walked to the top of the stairs at the end of the corridor, took hold of the handrail and, standing on tiptoe, leaned over as though scanning the street below. She stayed like that for a while; finally, with a look of resignation, she lowered herself down and returned to the flat. Kenta abandoned the idea of following the woman and clomped up the iron staircase in his wooden geta sandals.

He reached for the knob and turned it. The door opened easily.

'Mama?' called the little girl, coming to the door. Then, stopping short, she asked, 'Who're you?'

To his surprise, Kenta realised the girl could see him. 'Who're *you*?' he asked, turning the question back at her.

Nonplussed, the girl cocked her head to one side before answering.

'Kirara.'

'Come again?' asked Kenta, half teasingly.

'Ki–ra–ra,' the girl repeated.

'That's a funny name,' he said, drawing himself up with a supercilious air.

Kirara cocked her head again. It seemed a habit of hers. 'What's *your* name, Oniichan?' she asked him.

It rather pleased Kenta to hear the little girl address him as 'big brother' and he immediately felt kinder towards her. Kicking off his wooden geta, he leaned forward, half crouching, one arm outstretched with palm upraised, as he'd seen sideshow performers do, and proclaimed in a theatrical falsetto: 'Kenta "Sticky Fingers" Kusunoki at your service! Tokyo born'n'bred, I had my first bath in the sacred water of Kanda's Myojin Shrine and was raised in Ueno's notorious Piss Alley! And now you know who I am, pray tell me what I can do for you.'

When Kenta had finished this short oration, the girl stood stock-still and stared at him with wide eyes. After several moments of stunned silence, she began to slowly close the door.

'Wait!' he cried.

With his right foot Kenta snatched up one of his geta, grasping the thong between his toes, and shoved it against the door jamb a fraction of a second before the door shut. Wedged there, it acted as a doorstop. For a moment Kirara was too taken aback to react; Kenta meanwhile calmly opened the door and deftly slipped his outstretched toes into his geta and stepped back.

The girl shifted her gaze to Kenta's feet. Her intense stare made him self-conscious of his filthy sandals with their frayed fabric thongs and chipped edges.

When Kenta had run away from the orphanage for good, he'd meant to steal a pair of leather shoes, or at least some plimsolls, but there'd been none for the taking. So he settled for this pair of beat-up old geta, which at the time had seemed better than going barefoot.

Kirara was clearly fascinated by the curious objects. Finally, unable to contain her curiosity she pointed at Kenta's feet. 'What're *those*, Oniichan?'

'Oh, these?' The directness of the girl's question made Kenta realise perhaps he'd not chosen well after all. The geta *were* quite uncomfortable; their thongs, woven from a very stiff material, cut painfully into the soft skin in between his toes. 'Erm, you see, I had to skedaddle and these clomping things were all I could lay my mitts on,' he explained.

This pronouncement was greeted by another vacant look from Kirara, who had no clue what the boy was talking about.

Though he found her silence unsettling, Kenta was disinclined to leave. The girl reminded him of his younger sister whom he'd lost along with his parents in that big air raid in the spring of 1945, and he wondered where she might be now if she hadn't died. He was also powerfully drawn to Kirara's distinctive body odour, a mxture of dirt and sweat unique to people who have not bathed for some time. He knew the whiff of a comrade when he smelled one.

'Who was that cutie who came to the door just now?' he asked her.

He proceeded to describe the young woman he'd followed: her hair, clothes, even the handbag she'd been carrying.

Kirara's vacant expression suddenly vanished and her face lit up. 'Mama!' she cried, pushing open the door and rushing outside in her bare feet to scan the street below. Then she turned and raced back into the flat. She crossed the room to the balcony and hoisted herself onto the railing, locked her elbows, and, with her stomach pressed against the handrail, legs dangling in the air, gazed intently into the distance.

Finally, Kirara returned to the room and slumped down on the floor, dejected. Kenta was standing there too, having concluded there was no point lingering in the doorway.

'So she *was* your mum, huh?' He sounded sympathetic.

It was a great misfortune to lose one's parents. But it seemed an almost greater misfortune to be neglected by the one you had.

'I wonder why Mama doesn't come home,' mused Kirara. 'D'you s'pose she's lost? When *I* was lost I went to a policeman and he waited with me till she came 'n' found me.' Kirara said the word *policeman* in a tone that suggested a mixture of nostalgia and gratitude.

Kenta made a face and took a few steps back. 'You're joking!' he said incredulously. 'You oughta steer clear of the cops!

Kirara stared blankly at Kenta the way she did whenever he spoke. But since she could not think how to get him to leave, there he remained.

Kenta inspected the small room. On one side there was a metal clothes rack, a small white dressing table and a stack of plastic storage boxes with some soft toys and a make-up case on top. The floor was strewn with articles of women's clothing, buried among which were scraps of paper, discarded crisp packets and empty plastic drink bottles. A futon mattress had been left out on the floor, covered with the same sort of debris.

Kenta began hunting for plastic bottles; when he found one he unscrewed the cap, peered inside and gave it a sniff before tilting his head back and tipping the dregs into his mouth. Picking up food packages, he licked his fingers and used them to fish out any salt or crumbs at the bottom. But the emptiness in the pit of his stomach remained. There was nothing in the room capable of satisfying his hunger.

When Kenta was done he glanced at Kirara, who was regarding him enviously. 'Oh, did you want some? You shoulda said so,' he said, thinking if the little girl was hungry *she* could've done the same thing. But Kirara's innocent eyes – so much like his sister's – made him feel greedy for not sharing. Not that there'd been anything *worth* sharing. 'Sorry, kid,' he apologised, 'but my tank's been empty all morning.'

Kirara still looked at him but said nothing.

'As in my *fuel* tank, you know...' He patted his stomach and made a sad face.

For a while Kirara watched him. Then without a word she got up and went to the kitchen and began opening cupboards and taking out things. Seeing what she was up to, Kenta followed her to the kitchen and began opening boxes and looking inside jars.

When he'd examined everything, Kenta said, 'Well, kid, looks like we're in the same boat.'

Deciding it was useless staying there when there was nothing to eat, Kenta slipped on his geta and left the flat. Kirara trailed after him as he clomped his way down the iron staircase. At the bottom she ran and caught up with him and took his hand, as though nothing could be more natural. He turned his head and looked down at her. The little girl smiled back.

Kenta was glad he'd made an appearance that day.

LEADING KENTA BY THE HAND, Kirara headed for the local convenience store. In her free hand she held an envelope containing money. It wasn't much, just two thousand yen. Though too young to attend school, Kirara was old enough to understand it had to last her until her mother returned, or until another envelope arrived through the letter box.

The little girl walked through the store and carefully chose a discounted 1.5-litre bottle of Coca-Cola, a pack of biscuits with a long shelf-life and the largest bag of snack food from a pile next to the checkout, close to their sell-by date, which were 'priced to clear' at one hundred yen a piece.

Kirara approached the checkout and raised her items over her head and deposited them on the counter. The young woman behind the till, whose name tag read *Rey*, recoiled with an audible gasp and screwed up her face. Gingerly, she took the thousand-yen note which Kirara held out to her and put the girl's change and her receipt down on the counter, using her index finger to push them as far away as possible. She stopped short of holding her nose with her fingers, instead tucking in her chin and pulling up the collar of her work uniform so it covered her nose.

Accustomed to such treatment, no doubt, Kirara didn't seem to mind. Standing on tiptoe, she gathered up her loose change and grabbed the plastic bag containing her purchases. Then she paused and looked around, puzzled. Kenta, who had been with her a second ago, was gone. With both hands, she hauled up the bag containing the heavy Coke bottle and, trying her best to prevent it dragging on the ground, left the store.

Kenta was nowhere to be seen outside, either. Concluding the boy had abandoned her, Kirara started for home. But as soon as she'd turned the corner and was out of sight of the convenience store, Kenta stepped out from behind a telegraph pole. He'd stripped to the waist; slung over his shoulder was a bundle made from the grimy, too-large man's dress shirt he'd had on, the sleeves tied together as a strap. 'C'mon, kid, let's scram,' he said.

Kenta led the way back to Kirara's through back alleys and narrow passageways hemmed in on either side by boundary walls.

Kirara cleared off the low wooden table, sweeping the clutter onto the floor and replacing it with the plastic grocery bag containing the bottle of Coke, biscuits and snacks she'd bought at the store.

Kenta put down his own bundle and began removing the contents one at a time. There were tins of corned beef and mackerel cooked in miso sauce, seaweed-wrapped rice balls in assorted flavours, a bunch of bananas, and boxes of chocolates and milk toffees. Kirara's eyes practically popped out of her head as she took it all in.

The little girl gave Kenta such an awed look that it made him beam with satisfaction. When he smiled, Kirara could see one of his front teeth was missing. 'How...?' she faltered, eyeing the rice balls and chocolates longingly.

Kenta continued grinning without answering, so that Kirara, struck by a thought, reached for the envelope her mother had left her, which she'd tucked into her waistband before leaving the store, and carefully began counting out her change. *Now listen carefully, Kirara,* her mother had told her, *this is a five-hundred-yen coin, and this is a hundred … fifty yen, ten yen, one yen … If you forget, you won't eat,* she warned. By now Kirara could tell the coins apart pretty well but was less confident when it came to adding them up. So when her mother gave her money to spend, she constantly fretted about making a mistake.

'You can stop counting,' said Kenta, hurt that the little girl suspected him of robbing her. 'I don't need to steal from you. Didn't I tell you, in Ueno everyone called me "Sticky Fingers" Kenta?'

The truth was, no one in Ueno – or anywhere else – had ever called Kenta 'Sticky Fingers'. Hardly anyone called him anything at all, for that matter, not even his actual name. 'Sticky Fingers' was just a sobriquet Kenta dreamed up for himself after becoming a ghost. Over time, with each passing visit, he'd almost tricked himself into believing this little fiction of his was true.

'Where I come from,' he explained, 'a man doesn't steal from a young lady.'

Once again Kirara was completely lost and had no idea what the boy was going on about. But he opened a box of milk toffees, unwrapped a piece and popped it into his mouth, then took out another and tossed it to her. She fumbled it, picked it up and put it in her mouth; immediately her suspicions faded and she gazed at him as though he could do no wrong.

'I filched all this from that store,' he boasted.

In the years right after the war, when Kenta was living in the station underpass, a friend had given him a crash course in pickpocketing – a speciality of Tokyo's street children in those days. These pint-sized thieves, *charinko* as they were called, had been true artisans. But since becoming a ghost, Kenta could more or less steal with impunity, no skill required. He just went into a store and walked up to the cashier to check whether he was still invisible (and if they couldn't see him, they couldn't *smell* him, either). Once he knew that, he could go ahead and take whatever he liked.

'Anyway, let's tuck in – I'm starving!' Kenta tore the plastic wrapper off a rice ball and chomped down on it. Kirara must've been as hungry as he was, for she took the rice ball he tossed over to her and crammed it into her mouth with both hands. After they had wolfed down their food, they opened the bottle of Coca-Cola that Kirara had bought and quaffed glass after glass.

'Damn, it's been ages since I had rice *this* good!' crowed Kenta. He proceeded to peel a banana.

As soon as he'd eaten his fill, Kenta felt sleepy and lay down on the futon left spread out on the floor.

'Ah, what luxury!' he exclaimed. 'You sure are lucky to live in a swell place like this, kid.' Kenta frowned, remembering the station underpass he'd called home. He'd ended up there because there was no place else for him, and it had seemed as good a place as any. As far back as he could remember, right up until he was hit by the car, he'd only ever slept on a futon a handful of times at best, except for when his parents were still alive.

'You sure are lucky…' he repeated to himself as he closed his eyes.

Beside him, Kirara was already curled up in a ball, fast asleep.

WHEN KENTA OPENED HIS EYES, the sun was already quite high. He and Kirara split the remnants of the now-warm Coke and each stuffed one of Kirara's biscuits into their mouths. Then Kenta reached for the box of milk toffees, doling out one to himself and one to her.

'By the way, kid, you'd better not go back to that place again,' he warned, turning serious. 'As soon as they notice things're gone missing, they're bound to put two and two together and pin it on you. That chick was giving you funny looks, right? Go to a different store next time, when there're lots of other people around.'

Kenta thought he'd gladly have brought the little girl food anytime, if not for his fate which meant he'd be gone by the end of the day.

And what a pitiful fate it was! Kenta's infrequent visits to this mortal world were usually spent trying to assuage his craving for food. But no matter how much he ate it was never enough. Already the rice ball he'd just eaten seemed to have mysteriously vanished, leaving his stomach empty. Perhaps being a ghost meant he was incapable of satisfying his own alimentary cravings. But if the special ability death had given him enabled him to feed one person, this little girl, then wasn't he putting it to good use? Surely this one good deed outweighed his other sins. Of course, Kenta didn't frame it quite so philosophically in his own mind, but this was the essence of his thoughts.

But Kenta knew he'd be gone by the end of the day, and he worried lest the girl go back to the same store and find herself accused of shoplifting. Whenever some dirty child stinking to high heaven went into a store on their own and some goods went missing, they always got the blame, no matter how vociferously they denied it. Kenta had seen it happen time and again – kids who'd never stolen in their lives getting punched and kicked and turned over to the police. He didn't doubt the same would happen to Kirara.

Then, as he felt the last bit of caramelly sweetness slide off the back of his tongue and slither down his throat, Kenta had an idea.

'Hey, got any scissors?' he asked as he pressed another piece of milk toffee into Kirara's hand, after noticing her eyeing the box greedily.

'I'll get 'em,' she said, returning the sweet to its box and going to the kitchen.

'Let's give you a trim,' he said when she returned, taking the scissors from her. 'Girls look completely different with short hair.'

She looked at him uncomprehendingly.

Wading through piles of clothes and rubbish, Kenta led Kirara over to the white dressing table, sat her down facing the mirror and placed the scissors on the table.

Kenta ran his fingers through Kirara's long, greasy hair, sweeping it over the back of her head. Next, he picked up a plastic grocery bag lying nearby and pulled it over the flat, seaweed-like mass. Then, with his left hand, he grabbed the bag, holding tightly onto the hair inside, picked up the scissors in his right and began hacking away.

'Oh!' cried out Kirara in surprise at the sound of the scissors above her head.

Kenta went to the kitchen and crammed the plastic grocery bag full of Kirara's hair into the already overflowing trash bin. When he returned, large tears were streaming silently down the girl's face.

'W–what's the matter?' he stammered.

Kirara had liked her long hair and the loss of it came as a shock. But Kenta knew only the world of postwar Tokyo, where among Ueno's street children it had been normal for girls, for their own safety, to wear breeches and cut their hair short to pass as boys. Until he saw Kirara glaring at him with tearful eyes, it hadn't occurred to Kenta he was doing any harm.

After pacing around the cluttered room for a while wondering what to do, Kenta hit upon another idea. 'C'mon, kid,' he said, 'let's get you cleaned up.'

Surely the little girl would feel better after a good scrub from head to toe. And after a bath and a change of clothes – not to mention her new haircut – the convenience store woman would never recognise her as the stinky ragamuffin who'd come in before.

Kenta coaxed the reluctant little girl up from the chair and into the tiny bathroom, which he'd found on his earlier explorations. It had a foul odour all its own and was being used for storage. Kenta shifted some things someone had dumped in the tub over to the sink area before trying to turn on the tap. It was stiff, no doubt from long disuse, and it took all Kenta's strength to get it to budge. But no water came out.

'What the—?'

Kenta turned the tap a few more times but with the same result. Leaving Kirara in the bathroom he got up and went around trying the other taps, first in the sink area and then the kitchen.

'I'll be damned,' he said, clucking his tongue loudly. 'There's been a water cut!' What he couldn't have known was that the water – along with the gas and electricity – had been turned off because Kirara's mother had stopped paying the utility bill.

He tossed the things back into the tub and looked at Kirara. It would've been a stretch to have called Kirara's long hair pretty. But now, hacked off and uneven as it was, and still just as greasy, it wasn't surprising the little girl was unhappy with her new look.

'Well, since there's no water we'll just have to pop over to the ol' rub-a-dub-dub,' said Kenta.

Kirara cocked her head to one side.

'Well, if you step into that convenience store again smelling like this, you'll be in trouble. Plus, you'll feel better, I promise. C'mon, I know a place.'

Grabbing Kirara's hand, Kenta rushed out the door and down into the street.

'WOW, THIS PLACE NEVER CHANGES!' exclaimed Kenta.

Having raced down the hill and skipped along Ueno's main thoroughfare to Okachimachi, he and Kirara were now standing in front of an old bathhouse founded way back in 1950, the year before Kenta's death. Rarer still in this day and age, it was open in the morning.

'Now listen, kid,' explained Kenta excitedly, 'when you get inside hand your money to the woman behind the counter. Don't worry about me ... remember, she can't see me, so I don't pay. Then we'll go in together.'

Since becoming a ghost Kenta often went to the bathhouse, as there wasn't much else for him to do. One of the perks of being invisible was he could enter the women's bath if he wanted, though when it was crowded there was always the odd chance he might run into someone with heightened spiritual sensitivity. He'd come a cropper that way before and beat a hasty retreat without a stitch on him.

'Rub-a-dub-dub, rub-a-dub-dub,' Kirara repeated as she passed under the half-length curtain hanging in the doorway. Although she still hadn't quite grasped what was going on, she found Kenta's high spirits infectious.

From behind the counter a woman in her sixties peered down at Kirara though a pair of spectacles perched at the end of her nose. 'You all on your own?' she asked.

Kirara started to shake her head 'no' when Kenta, standing just behind her, reached forwards and forced her head down.

'Your mum and dad send you?'

This time, without any prompting from Kenta, Kirara nodded her head and said, 'Uh-huh.'

'My, but you stink, don't you!' exclaimed the woman. 'Go in there like that and you'll drive my customers away.' Then, turning her head, she called out, 'Hey,

Sumi ... you there?' At this, a somewhat younger woman – possibly her daughter – appeared from the back. 'Sumi, take this little girl in and give her a good scrub, would you? Only, do it off to the side, as there's another customer in there right now. Use a facecloth and throw it away afterwards. Don't let her into the tub until she's good and clean. Got it?' When the woman was done giving Sumi these instructions, she turned her attention back to Kirara. 'Now, I must warn you, our bathwater's piping hot ... so don't go jumping in!' she said, wagging a finger at the girl. 'Scoop some out of the tub into one of those bowls and pour it over yourself a little at a time, then ease yourself in nice and slow. Understand?' Then she turned back to Sumi and said, in a casual tone, as though Kirara wasn't there, 'I mean, we can't turn her away just 'cos she's filthy, now can we? This is a bathhouse after all ... and if there's one thing this poor child needs, it's some soap and hot water!' Then, peering down again at Kirara through her spectacles, she asked, 'Got any money?'

Kirara tipped some loose change out of the envelope her mother had given her. The woman took a five-hundred-yen coin and handed Kirara back four hundred and twenty yen in change. Suddenly, the woman looked fixedly past Kirara, as if something behind the little girl had just caught her attention. Fearing she'd sensed his presence, Kenta stole swiftly over to the entrance of the men's bath and ducked into the changing room.

It was an in-between time of day, when people were getting ready to go to work, and the men's bath was empty. Kenta sat down on a stool, lathered himself from head to toe using the liquid soap provided, and rinsed off with the shower nozzle. Then, taking advantage of the fact he was alone, he went to the edge of the large tub and cannonballed in. 'Yikes – it's hot!' he cried, springing right back out.

This process was repeated several times before Kenta managed to immerse himself up to his neck. After a bit, he began paddling round in circles.

The sliding door to the changing room rattled open and a man entered. Kenta quickly moved to the edge of the tub, lifted himself halfway out, resting his bottom on the rim, and scooted slowly over to one side, keeping only his feet in the water. When another man came in, he seized his chance: he raced towards the door, skidding across the wet floor, and slipped through into the changing room. Dressing quickly, he went out, but Kirara had not yet appeared.

While Kenta waited, he amused himself by sticking out his lower lip and sending puffs of air out of his mouth and across his face. After a few minutes, Kirara emerged from the women's side of the bathhouse accompanied by Sumi. The little girl's fringe was tied up in a topknot with a pink rubber band and she wore an adult-sized T-shirt that came down to her knees; Kirara's dress had been so filthy, presumably Sumi hadn't wanted to put her back in it. With her face sparkling clean, Kirara looked very pretty indeed and the two women seemed delighted at the result of their handiwork.

'See,' said Kenta, 'told ya you'd feel better after a bath.'

The older woman actually came out from behind the counter to see Kirara off and even went so far as to buy her a chilled can of Pocari Sweat from the vending machine outside the front door. At this Sumi laughed and said, 'Eighty yen for the bath and a hundred for the drink ... where's the profit in that!' to which the older woman shot back, 'Don't forget the T-shirt; now that's what you call VIP service!' and then to Kirara: 'You come again anytime you like, dear ... just don't wait till you get so dirty!'

Kirara smiled affably and waved goodbye. After his hot bath, the cool sports drink was a revelation to Kenta. 'Man, this stuff is amazing!' he exclaimed. 'Sweet *and* salty!'

They sauntered back towards Ueno, taking turns sipping the refreshing beverage. When they reached the Ameyoko shopping area near the station, Kenta recounted, 'Back in my time, this was all a black market. You could find *anything* here, and the place reeked of stew made from the GIs' leftovers; me and my friends, we used to pick pockets, sell re-rolled cigarettes and shine shoes. When it got dark, we'd bed down for the night in the underpass. There were so many people down there, it didn't feel all that cold even in winter.'

Kenta's feet naturally led him to the station underpass. As he walked, talking to Kirara, vivid memories of those times came flooding back; falling silent, he leaned back against a wall and slowly sank to the cool concrete floor. Copying him, Kirara sat down beside him. People walked briskly by in both directions, taking no notice of the two children, or rather of the little girl sitting by herself.

Kenta reached into his back pocket and took out a box of milk toffees. He gave one to Kirara and popped one into his mouth. There was a time when such largesse would have been unthinkable. But now stealing had become so easy there was no reason to be stingy; besides, he was going to get hit by a car that evening anyway.

'I'm going to die today, kid,' said Kenta on an impulse. Kirara did not react.

'You see, I saw a sweet potato lying in the road,' he continued. 'Someone must've dropped it. I dashed out to grab it before some other kid spotted it. I never saw the car coming…'

'Did it hurt?' asked Kirara.

'I don't know … I can't remember. But it's going to happen again.'

Kirara cocked her head to one side in that way of hers.

'Whatever you do, kid, don't follow me … or you'll get run over too.'

''Kay,' Kirara nodded.

Kenta deftly folded his square toffee wrapper into a paper aeroplane and threw it. The tiny missile flew a surprising distance before falling to the floor.

'Make me one too!' entreated Kirara, proffering her wrapper.

'Make it yourself. Here, lemme teach you … First, fold the wrapper in half and crease it down the middle. Next, fold here and here to make two triangles. Now, fold the triangles in half…'

But Kirara's fingers were clumsy; try as she might, the two sides turned out lopsided.

'The wrapper's too small,' said Kenta, consolingly. 'We'll try with a bigger piece of paper next time.' He took the wrapper from Kirara's hand. In the blink of an eye he refolded it into another perfect, tiny aeroplane and handed it to her. 'Here, try throwing it,' he said. Gripping the plane in her little fingers, Kirara tossed it into the air. It dipped and nosedived straight into the ground. 'You gotta aim the tip up. That way it'll arc a bit and fly straight.' Kenta demonstrated by throwing the plane a few more times. Each time the plane arced gracefully through the air and sailed straight. Kirara abandoned the idea of throwing the paper plane herself and instead begged Kenta to do it again and again.

The two came out of the passageway onto the street and climbed the long flight of steps leading into the park, Kirara tottering ahead and pulling Kenta along by the hand.

'Wait, kid, we shouldn't go in here ... there're supposed to be pervs all over the place,' Kenta protested. 'They'll stick their thing up your rear end,' he warned.

But Kirara led Kenta to a large plaza bustling with people and immediately his misgivings vanished and his high spirits returned.

'Wow! Whaddya suppose is going on today? Maybe it's the Obon flower market...'

It was in fact the day of the annual Japanese azalea festival. The plaza was lined on both sides with stalls, like at a temple fair, displaying row upon row of bonsais covered with bright, colourful blossoms. The two children walked around inspecting the miniature trees.

'Whoa, get a load of this baby!' Kenta exclaimed, walking up to one as tall as him. 'It's gotta be the biggest bonsai ever!' Even Kirara laughed.

The two children moved on towards a large fountain and sat down nearby. Soon they were sprawled out on their backs gazing up at a cloudless blue sky.

'This place is huge,' said Kenta.

The sky loomed high above their heads.

Tired after their hot baths, the two children started to feel sleepy again. Before long they had dozed off.

'I KNEW RIGHT AWAY your mum was from around here,' said Kenta. 'Ueno whores aren't like those ones downtown in Yurakucho,' he opined. He and his fellow street urchins proudly referred to Ueno's prostitutes as 'cuties' and derided Yurakucho's streetwalkers as 'hags'.

This was in response to Kirara, who in dribs and drabs had begun to tell him about her mother.

Kirara's mum had lived with her once, occasionally going out at night and not returning till the next morning. These days, though, the little girl never knew from one day to the next when her mother might turn up. Twice before now, Kirara had found an envelope with money in it stuck through the letter box. Sometimes a scary man came and pounded on the door demanding his 'dough'.

Kenta pictured Kirara's mother as he'd seen her that morning. Even with all that make-up on she'd seemed quite young, and he guessed she couldn't have been much more than a child herself when Kirara was born.

Back in his day, he'd seen many girls barely older than himself with 'a bun in the oven', as they said.

Kenta took out a leaflet he'd picked up at the azalea festival and folded it diagonally into a triangle, with a leftover bit at the edge which he folded over and creased with his fingernail before tearing it away. Then he unfolded the triangle and showed it to Kirara.

'See, I've made a square,' he said. 'Now, just fold it in half like before, then make two triangles and fold it here and here. The next step is important ... if you don't fold it right it won't fly.'

Unlike the tiny paper plane made from the milk toffee wrapper, the big wings of Kirara's new paper aeroplane caught the wind and soared up, up into the air, gliding unobstructed across the open space of the park.

'Do it again!' Kirara shouted, delighted.

The park was full of fun things to do. Kenta and Kirara chased one another, climbed on the bronze statues and played with a toy panda Kenta stole from one of the kiosks near the zoo.

For the first time in her life, Kirara folded a paper plane all by herself, from start to finish, and sent it sailing through the air, happily chasing it all over. Kenta, for the first time since becoming a ghost, wished he could remain in this world just a bit longer.

Kirara's paper plane soared up into the air and away from the fountain, towards the big museum across the street, and she raced blindly after it.

Suddenly, there was a flash of blue and a screech of brakes, then someone slammed into her with a thud and sent her sprawling onto the pavement in front of the entrance to the museum.

A grown-up got out of the blue car and asked if she was hurt. As passers-by clustered around her, Kirara jerked her head around and stared at the body lying broken and crumpled in the road.

A Special Day

KAYA FELT SHE WAS IN some strange kind of limbo, having just settled into the women's student dorm and now waiting for lectures to start. She had no acquaintances in her new environment, and nobody here knew who she was. There had to be some former students from her high school somewhere in this big city, but she didn't know any well enough to pay a visit. Her mother had told her not to waste money and she wanted to get a part-time job as soon as possible, but the academic year hadn't yet officially started and she wasn't aware that she could find work through the student affairs office. And so she passed the time in a daze.

Her room in the dorm had a small kitchen and bathroom, furnished with a bed, a desk, a couple of cheap shelf units, a refrigerator, and a space to put a washing machine. The reason it was just a space was that the machine hadn't been delivered yet. It would be convenient to be able to do her laundry in her room, Kaya thought. She also had the option of arranging to have breakfast and dinner in the dorm canteen, which boasted a nutritionist to ensure the meals were balanced.

For the first few days she'd eaten all her meals there. The orientation for new students wouldn't take place until mid-month, so she didn't even know who were freshers and who were returning students, and being too shy to introduce herself to anyone she had quietly eaten her meals and then hurried back to her room.

Still, it would be crazy to remain cooped up in her room all day, so she made a point of going out every day after breakfast to begin exploring the better known areas of the city. The nearest station was about a ten-minute walk from the dorm. The area was residential and poorly lit at night, which didn't feel all that safe, but the dorm prided itself on its strict security and had never experienced any safety issues.

The first place Kaya visited was Harajuku. Next she went to Daikanyama and Jiyugaoka. She didn't know which parts of Shibuya were safe to walk in, so she only went to the 109 department store there. She wandered around Ueno Park and visited the great temple in Asakusa. She went to Shinjuku, too, although she didn't like it very much.

She wanted to browse the book stores in Jinbocho and decided to walk there, but walked and walked without coming across anything even vaguely resembling the description. She must have taken a wrong turn somewhere, despite constantly checking the map.

She had never been any good at following maps and was always getting lost. Maybe she'd been roaming around the less touristy parts of Harajuku, Daikanyama and Ueno, since she hadn't found them all that exciting.

She ticked off the places she visited in the guidebook, but had failed more than once or twice to find places or shops she'd intended to go to. She wasn't really bothered about it, though. After all, she was on her own and didn't have any particular goal in mind. And she would be living here for at least four years, so she needn't rush to see everything all at once. She would get to know the city little by little.

Since she was simply wandering at her leisure she didn't mind if she took some wrong turns, but this time she was growing a little uneasy. However far she walked, all she saw was office buildings. It was starting to get tedious. She was beginning to think that if she didn't stop now and go back the way she'd come, she would never find her way home. She didn't yet know Tokyo well enough to be familiar with the metro and bus routes, and the thought that she'd be in trouble if she got lost now began to weigh on her. She should ask a passer-by for directions to the nearest station, Kaya thought. But she couldn't even see anyone out on the street.

Turning into an alley, she caught sight of something strange.

It was an old stone building with its arched entrance covered in a relief of owls, sheep, rabbits and other animals, and two stone guardian lions standing either side. Kaya looked up and saw that the upper floors were constructed in brick. She could make out the word *Building* written in katakana from right to left, the old-fashioned way, but the rest of the name was no longer legible. Still, there was a sheet of paper with the word *Gallery* pasted next to the entrance, so she assumed it was open to the public. The door had glass panels and a brass handle, and there was a heavy-looking plate embedded in the wall that read *Important Cultural Property*.

Kaya completely forgot about finding a station and peered through the glass at the interior. An old man on reception dressed like a hotel doorman in a gold-striped uniform and cap smiled broadly at her and waved to indicate she should enter. Seeing her hesitate, he made a point of coming to open the door for her. 'Please, do come in,' he said, then added pleasantly, almost imploringly, 'Isn't this place wonderful?'

'Mmm,' Kaya responded vaguely.

'In the old days there used to be quite a few buildings like this around here, you know. There aren't many left now, though. Feel free to look around. We do ask that you don't take any photographs, though.'

'Is that your uniform?' Kaya blurted out.

'No,' the old man answered flatly. 'These are my own clothes. But they suit this building well, don't you think? I was a guard in another place for a very long time, and I feel like I'm getting a second lease of life in this job. I was told to wear regular clothes to work, but that felt just too dull, so I had this outfit specially made.'

'I think it suits you,' Kaya said to flatter him. The old man beamed at her, evidently pleased.

'What floor is the gallery on?' She glanced up at the ceiling and saw a smallish but splendid chandelier.

The old man pressed a button with an up arrow beside a sturdy, old-fashioned elevator. 'There are galleries on every floor. Take the lift up to the top floor and work your way down.' He smiled again. 'After all, if I'm going to do something again, I might as well do something I like,' he said quickly as the door closed on Kaya.

The elevator came to life with a roar of machinery, and the heavy box moved slowly upwards. Upon reaching the top floor, there was a loud clang, like a bell being struck, and the door opened.

Kaya felt disorientated as she stepped out into the corridor. She couldn't see anything resembling a gallery. The doors looked like the ones you saw in old Japanese films which normally had company names stencilled on them in black or white paint, but the doors here were all just plain wood with no name or any sign at all. Surely none of these could be galleries – and even if they were, they wouldn't be the sort of place a young student fresh from the sticks could just walk in, she thought. She was about to head for the stairs when one of the doors opened and a woman stuck her head out. And there inside the door was indeed a sign saying *Gallery* and she could even see some of the exhibits.

The woman was wearing a bright red blouse and a white polka-dot skirt. Her hair was dyed a bright orangey red and she was wearing red tortoiseshell glasses. As their eyes met, the woman said amiably, 'I don't suppose you were intending to come here, were you?'

Before Kaya could reply the woman indicated with her head that she should come in. Kaya could have made her escape down the staircase, but she couldn't think of any reason why she shouldn't go into the gallery.

The space inside was enclosed by plain white walls, and a number of cubes were scattered about, upon which sat artworks ranging from a pot, an animal, and even something resembling a spaceship. Everything was in pastel shades, like clouds of cherry and wisteria blossoms.

The artworks were simply numbered and the overall theme of the exhibition appeared to be 'A Special Day'. A panel at the entrance read:

> All the works here were originally created for an exhibition by a certain artist, but were damaged en route to the gallery in an accident. Some of the artist's friends had the idea of creating 'A Special Day' for all these works that were robbed of life before seeing the light of day, so that they may be reborn just once before being thrown away. His friends pieced together the fragments of the damaged works, covered them in a special fibre, and painted them for this exhibition.

Items further in had been draped with white cloths. It was apparently closing time.

'I'm sorry we have to close now, just when you'd taken the trouble to come here,' the woman with red hair and matching glasses told Kaya apologetically as she held out a sheet of paper. It looked like a leaflet about the building's galleries. 'Today's the last day, and the transporters will be here soon, so I have to get everything ready. Are you an art student?' she asked abruptly.

Kaya shook her head emphatically.

'Oh really? You did do well to find us, then. Anyway, I think the other exhibitions will still be open for a while, so do pay them all a visit. I'm sure you'll find something to interest you. Can I have that back a moment?' She took the leaflet, picked a red pen out of the desk, and circled something. 'There's an opening party at five, so do come along.'

Kaya shook her head again, but the woman looked at her quizzically. 'You don't need an invitation, and there'll be drinks and refreshments provided, too.'

Kaya thanked her and slipped out of the door, her footsteps echoing through the old building.

From outside, she hadn't realised that were so many gallery spaces inside. The gallery names had the respective room numbers noted next to them on the leaflet, and on the ground floor there was also a café, bookshop, and a small shop selling stationery and other knick-knacks.

Kaya wondered why they didn't have a sign up outside the building to advertise the spaces inside. Maybe it was meant to be a hip space that only those in the know would come to.

There was another gallery on the next floor down, so she cautiously opened the door and was taken aback to see a solitary man asleep in an empty space. She looked at the leaflet to see what exhibition was taking place here, and read, 'Installation: Creative Time'. She quietly closed the door, wondering whether this really was an installation, or whether some homeless guy had snuck in for a nap.

'Don't go!' came an anguished cry, and the sleeping man jumped up and came after her. 'I've been doing this all day, but only one person actually came in. Why?' Kaya didn't know how to answer this and was lost for words. 'Well, it doesn't really matter,' the man went on. 'You don't have to say anything. I just thought maybe I'd better explain. "Creative Time" is ... how can I put it? Just to look at it, you wouldn't think what it's showing is creative at all.'

The man didn't look much older than Kaya herself. He was wearing torn jeans, white Converse sneakers, and a scruffy threadbare waistcoat over a T-shirt.

'Did I look as though I was asleep?' He stood blocking Kaya's way so she couldn't escape. 'I did, didn't I? I was supposed to. After all, it's "Creative Time". An aunt of mine is a novelist and she's always napping during the day. But she isn't actually asleep, she says. While she's lying down not moving, inspiration wells up in her, becomes a dream, and goes rushing freely round and round her head. The moment she wakes up from the dream, she gets up and writes it all down before she forgets it. Of course it isn't a proper story at that stage, but it gives her something to work with. So I wanted to try it for myself. It's not real sleep, you know. And then I had an idea. I mean, why not make myself into an installation that other people can observe? I've been doing it for the last three days, but people always open the door, see me, and run away.'

Kaya smiled vaguely and slipped past him, heading for the stairs, but he followed after her talking nineteen to the dozen.

'Hey, are you coming to the opening party on the ground floor later?' he called down the stairs after her. 'It's at five, and anyone can come!'

Kaya answered noncommittally, wondering why everyone was so keen on getting her to come to the party, and ducked into a room on the next floor to get away from him. This space appeared to be a photography exhibition. She'd felt enticed to come in here, but the photographs themselves weren't exactly appealing. The title was 'Self/Presence', and all featured the same man pulling a terrifying face. The photographs weren't bad, but the man was so annoying that she wanted to photoshop him out of all of them. She just couldn't really get this notion of making yourself into art, neither in this exhibition or the previous one.

Still, it would have been so much better if the other man she'd encountered just now had been the one in the photographs, she thought suddenly, surprising herself. It appeared that she quite liked the 'Creative Time' man, but not the 'Self/Presence' one.

The photos showed the 'Self/Presence' man making a scary face in landscapes all over Japan, but there was just one in which the scenery looked familiar and stopped her in her tracks. Of course, the other photos featured scenery she recognised, like Mount Fuji or the Tokyo Skytree, but this particular one looked like it had been taken on a remote beach in the area she herself was from.

It wasn't a well-known location and there was nothing special about the beach, so there was no reason for the photographer to have been there other than it was clearly a place he knew. Kaya imagined herself on the beach in place of the man. She could almost smell the sea air she loved so much.

She left the exhibition and went into a gallery displaying some rather quaint traditional Japanese washi paper. It was apparently the collection of a washi artist, and the delicate forms of flowers, grasses, and kanji characters could be seen embedded within the paper.

There were already some other people in the gallery, a woman wearing a no-nonsense white blouse with grey cropped trousers, and a girl about the same age as Kaya with short bobbed hair and dressed in a kimono. Kaya thought she must be the artist since she'd gone to the trouble of wearing a kimono.

The woman in a white blouse moved away to answer her phone, and the girl smiled at Kaya. 'This feels so nostalgic, doesn't it? I've always wanted to come somewhere like this all dressed up, just for once.'

Kaya was somewhat bewildered at suddenly being spoken to like this, but the girl took her hand and said, 'You're a student, right?'

She herself was just about to start at some university in Tokyo, in Mejiro or somewhere. But there happened to be a couple in this neighbourhood who were long-standing family friends she could rely on for help if needed, so she had decided to find digs nearby. Wouldn't Kaya like to come and see her place?

'You mean now?'

'That's right. I'm Miya Watanabe. What are you called?'

'Kaya Watanabe.'

'Hey, our names are almost the same!'

'Are you the artist?' said Kaya, finally asking the question that had been on her mind. Miya shook her head and explained vaguely that she'd simply wanted to come somewhere like this and so here she was.

She headed for the stairs, still holding Kaya's hand. Kaya thought she was being a bit pushy given that she hadn't agreed to go, but she felt strangely reassured to know they were both about to start at university, and since she had nothing better to do she went along with her.

Miya opened a heavy door on the opposite side of the building from the one through which Kaya had entered. There was no sign of the old man who had talked to her earlier. The door opened onto a well-maintained interior garden, and as they walked past white spirea, golden forsythia, and azaleas all in bloom, Kaya wondered what had become of that built-up office district she'd been walking through earlier.

Still pulling Kaya by the hand, Miya moved quickly through the front entrance of a high-rise apartment block. As Miya released the autolock and they got into the lift, Kaya thought how different it was from her dorm room.

'Well then, come along in,' Miya said, waving her into a studio flat that comprised a minimally furnished tatami room with a low wooden table and two floor seats. It was more reminiscent of an inn at a hot springs resort than a young woman's apartment. What's more, the far end of the room was a glass wall with a view of a pond, trees, and sky. It really did feel like a luxury hotel room.

'How come?'

'What do you mean?'

'I mean, how come you can't see any buildings from here.'

'It's on a hill – it's designed that way,' Miya said dismissively.

'Oh come on, it's the sort of room you'd want to bring a guy back to, isn't it?' Kaya said, astonished that she had said such a thing.

'Really?' Miya said as she poured some coffee. 'I haven't done so yet.'

'So why don't you, then?' Kaya said. For some reason she felt terribly daring, sitting there enveloped in the aroma of coffee. It must be because she was with someone she didn't know. It occurred to her that with her new lifestyle here in the city, she was probably going to be much more adventurous than she had been back home in the countryside.

'Sure. Shall we go to the opening party and pick up a man we both like and bring him back here?' Miya said mischievously. Kaya laughed with her. 'After all, I wanted to see what it was like to live somewhere like this, and I feel like today I can do whatever I like,' Miya went on confidently. 'Today really feels like a special day, doesn't it? Don't you feel that too? Let's go find someone and bring him here!'

'You go for it if you like, Miya,' Kaya said, a little awkwardly.

'I guess. At least you guys still have time,' Miya said.

What a weird thing to say, Kaya thought uncomfortably. For one thing, it sounded like Miya was stressing how different the two of them were. And what was it with the way she'd said 'you guys' in the plural?

Miya went to touch up her make-up, then the two of them went back through the garden to the other building. The sun hadn't yet gone down but it was already getting chilly. They went past the old elevator and out the front entrance, then headed around the building to the party venue. There were already quite a lot of people there, queuing alongside the building looking bored as they waited for the venue to open.

'What's the exhibition?' Kaya asked Miya.

'Not sure, but I think it's about dolls.'

'Dolls?'

'It's open,' Miya said and, as if avoiding Kaya's question, joined the surge of people entering the venue. Left on her own, Kaya also made her way in.

Inside there were a number of dolls with white porcelain skin. Some were dressed in clothes of white lace yellowed with age, while others were naked. As the woman in red glasses had promised, there were glasses of champagne and orange juice, crackers with cheese and salmon, and fruit. Looking around she saw the woman in red glasses and the uniformed old man. The woman who had been talking with Miya in the gallery was also there, drink in hand.

'Ladies and gentlemen,' began a tall man, apparently the doll maker, raising his glass.

Kaya suddenly realised that everyone around her was already holding a drink, so after a moment's hesitation, she picked up a glass of champagne. She didn't think anyone here would bother to check her age.

'I am truly honoured that so many people have gathered here today for the opening of my exhibition. It has been my dream to some day unveil my work to you. On this special day, I am deeply thankful to have the opportunity of meeting you all. Today is the day my dream has come true.'

Maybe this was the doll maker's first exhibition, Kaya mused as she listened to his speech. And Miya Watanabe had said something similar earlier, she recalled.

'When a sculptor of Buddhist images carves a statue,' the doll maker went on, 'he uses his chisel to carve out the soul latent in the wood, and I believe we doll makers feel the same way about our work. In other words, we do not pull our creations out of thin air, we merely help to give form to something that already exists so that everyone can see it. I created each and every piece you see here today with precisely this sentiment. *Some day I will exhibit them*, I thought ... I once gave up on the idea, but finally it has come to pass. I am overwhelmed with emotion.'

He choked up and an elderly woman – a friend maybe, or the gallery owner – took over and proposed a toast. As everyone in the venue raised their glasses, he once again took the microphone and resumed his speech.

'And all doll makers probably share a dream that once a year – or even just once a decade – the day will surely come when all the dolls achieve a soul and come to life with blood coursing through them, and begin to speak. And I do think it's possible something like this could happen on a special day like today, I really do.'

The venue erupted with angry shouts: 'You mustn't do anything like that! It's against the rules!' 'Impossible. It could never happen!' 'How dare you put dolls on the same level as people!' 'What's so wrong about it? Do it!'

'Quiet please, quiet!' the doll maker said. 'I'm just daydreaming. I would never seriously wish for it.'

The crowd settled down again. The elderly woman told everyone to enjoy themselves and to take their time looking around. Kaya felt someone nudge her elbow. She turned to see a familiar-looking man standing there. She smiled vaguely, wracking her brains to remember who he was, and then gave a little cry of surprise.

'What's wrong?' he asked calmly.

'You're the Self/Something guy!'

'Self/Presence.'

The man seemed extraordinarily pleased by Kaya's reaction. In other words, he had taken her reaction as evidence she had seen his exhibition, and nothing could make an artist happier – and what's more, he seemed to have no doubt whatsoever that she had appreciated it.

'So, how come you're in all of the photos?' Kaya asked, her tongue loosened by the champagne,

'Because that is Self/Presence,' he said confidently, as though that explained everything.

You can't say anything to a man like this, Kaya thought, and decided to change tack.

'One of the photos is of the countryside where I'm from. By the sea in Wakayama.'

'Everyone has the same reaction. That's what I aimed for.'

'It is?'

'Everyone who views the exhibition will find one photo that looks like where they are from. That's the sort of exhibition I wanted to hold – and it seems I succeeded!'

'It seems I succeeded?' What an irresponsible, random thing to say, Kaya thought.

'That's Self/Presence,' he repeated calmly.

I do wish he'd left himself out of it though, Kaya thought again, although she didn't say so. Noting her lack of enthusiasm the man slipped away, parting the sea of people as he went.

Kaya walked past the row of dolls, examining each one in turn.

Their unseeing eyes were staring straight ahead, and they looked as though they had something to say. With her head muddled by the champagne, she was beginning to lose her ability to distinguish between dolls and people. She wasn't used to alcohol and hadn't realised that even just a little could get her quite drunk.

She heard a commotion across the room and idly glanced that way to see the young 'Creative Time' man shouting. Looking around the venue, she caught sight of Self/Presence and Miya Watanabe gaily slipping out the door holding hands.

Surely not, she thought tipsily. Of all the men Miya could have chosen as the first to take back to her beautiful room, he was the one she chose? She suddenly recalled Miya and the Self guy having their picture taken, with Miya laughing and him pulling his trademark scary face.

She heard the sound of a glass breaking, and people started crying 'Stop that now!' and 'Pull yourself together!' The next moment, Creative Time was rushing towards her – although of course he was simply heading for the exit, and Kaya just happened to be slumped on the floor next to it.

'What's up with you?' he asked her.

'I'm a bit drunk.'

'I'm leaving now.'

'Then take me with you. I don't know where the station is.'

In her drunken haze, Kaya did her best to focus and grabbed his arm. Looking resigned, he pulled her up.

'I don't know what the hell those guys were on,' he grumbled on the way to the station. 'They were all saying things like, "I've always wanted to do this", and "Today's the day to do it!" All I said was, I still don't know what it is I most want to do, and they all started attacking me. I mean, what the hell? Why should I get beaten up for saying something like that? I mean, it's normal, right? I'm still young.'

As he went on and on, Kaya's head gradually began to clear.

'Were the people hitting you older than you?'

'No, not at all! If anything, one of them might even have been younger. When I said I'd been here for three days, he yelled at me demanding to know why. And then everyone started yelling. Three days is against the rules! That sort of thing. What rules, dammit? I paid the gallery fee.'

'Was the rule for everyone else just for today?' Kaya asked, thinking that actually Creative Time was just her type. If she had a posh flat like Miya's she might even take him home with her – but, as it was, she could hardly take him back to the women's dorm.

'Isn't it weird to hold an opening party when there's a "Today only" rule in place?'

Creative Time carried on complaining right up until the metro station sign came into sight.

'Here's the station. Do you know how to get home from here?' he asked dubiously.

'Sure,' she said, then wished she'd said no so he'd have to offer to see her back to the dorm. Still, she was too shy to correct herself.

They said goodbye and Kaya went to get her train. It really was odd to have an opening party for an exhibition held for one day only, she thought, and went to check the leaflet the woman in red glasses had given her, but she must have dropped it somewhere.

THE NEXT FEW WEEKS were really busy for Kaya. With the start of the academic year, her head was full of registering for classes, attending orientations, and so forth. For a while her time was taken up going back and forth between the university and the dorm, then there was the social gathering for the languages class and events introducing the various student clubs. It was all fun in its own way.

One day soon after the Golden Week spring holiday, on a sudden whim she got on a train and went back to where that building had been. Not having any sense of direction, however, she was completely unable to find it. She thought the high-rise apartment where Miya Watanabe lived might provide a convenient landmark, but she couldn't find any trace of the places she'd seen that day.

She couldn't blame it entirely on having been drunk, and she was beginning to feel that everything that happened had all been a dream. Or that for some reason the people she'd met could only appear on that one day, like the dolls brought to life for that day only.

Turning a corner with her head full of such thoughts, she caught sight of a cosy-looking café that somehow drew her to it.

The entire front of the café was large glass sliding doors that opened onto the street. The glass was old and uneven, but the overall effect was more modern than quaint. The large interior held a miscellaneous assortment of tables and chairs, coffee tables, sofas, and leafy plants. At the back, next to a spiral staircase, there was a kitchen and a counter, where a young woman with her hair pulled back in a ponytail was operating an espresso machine.

Kaya went closer and looked inside, then gave a start. Wasn't that Creative Time wearing the café's house apron and going around taking orders?

She slid a door open and went in.

'Table for one?' Creative Time asked. Apparently he hadn't recognised her.

'Yes,' she replied. He smiled at her good-naturedly and told her to sit wherever she liked.

While she waited for her order of a coffee and a piece of Swiss roll, she couldn't shake off a nagging feeling of trying to remember something but being unable to. She thought of grabbing Creative Time and asking him about that day, but decided not to. She'd rather gaze at him while he worked, she realised. And now that she knew where he worked, she began to think it would be better to take her time over getting to know him.

Just as Creative Time brought her delicious-smelling cup of coffee, Kaya finally remembered what Miya had said that day.

At least you guys still have time.

The Pet Civet

SAYA PUSHED OPEN THE GATE and went into the garden, which was overgrown with clover, purple vetch, and shepherd's purse. Numerous flowers were blooming, though nobody was there to appreciate them. Cherry blossoms were beginning to scatter, and persimmon buds were just peeking out. It was a riot of luxuriant trees, with maple, magnolia, windmill palm, camellia, loquat, plum and bitter summer orange, and creeping vines entwining their way up to the roof of the house.

Her aunt's single-storey wooden cottage was on the small side, but the property itself was a more or less decent size if you included the small vegetable garden beyond the fence.

Fifty years had passed since the cottage was built, and the front door and storm shutters were not exactly easy to open. It took some pushing and pulling and bashing before Saya finally managed to open the windows and let in some fresh air. Her aunt had died a month and a half earlier, but including the time she'd spent in hospital she had been away for nearly three months, and the house was extremely dusty. Saya intended to dispose of all her aunt's belongings so there was no need to clean the place now, but she found it hard to breathe and so decided to run the vacuum over it. Everyone had assumed that it would never have occurred to her aunt when she'd fallen ill and gone to hospital that she would not be returning, but the place was so neat and tidy that Saya had to think she'd been well-prepared.

A pleasant breeze came in from the veranda as she wiped down the tatami mats in the living room with a damp cloth. After clearing away the bucket she'd used for the cleaning, she went back into the living room, then froze.

There was someone sitting on the veranda.

'Who are you?' demanded Saya.

'Who are you?' the young man retorted indignantly. He was wearing a beige cardigan over his white collarless shirt, dark brown corduroy trousers, and work boots.

Saya was under no obligation to answer questions from a suspicious stranger. 'How did you get in?' she pressed him.

'Through the garden. The gate isn't locked, and anyway it's normal in the countryside. That's what the veranda's for, so visitors don't have to come in the front door.'

'What are you doing here?'

'I was in the area, so dropped by. I thought I would pay a farewell visit.'

'You shouldn't just let yourself in like this.'

'What about you?'

'I'm the owner of this property.'

'The owner died last month.'

'I'm her niece. I inherited it.'

'Really? Well, in that case, you could say I'm something like a nephew.'

The man spoke quietly, but was clearly not about to back down.

He looked to be in his late twenties, and had clean-cut features with a straight nose. From the way he was dressed he didn't appear to be employed in a typical company, but there was an air about him that was out of place in a rural house during working hours on a weekday.

'Nephew?'

'Well, something like that.'

'I've never heard about any nephew before, and how come you weren't at the funeral?'

'I didn't know about the funeral,' the man said.

Confused, Saya sat down.

Her aunt had been the younger sister of Saya's stepfather. She'd never married and had worked in a credit union in Kofu until retirement. After their parents died she'd bought this house in rural Yamanashi and had lived here alone growing vegetables in the garden. She didn't have anything to do with any of her relatives, who generally regarded her as an eccentric.

Saya's mother Masayo had been single when she'd had Saya, and the two had lived alone until Masayo met Yoichiro Hanawa. Yoichiro was older by twenty years, and married at the time. When he left his wife and moved in with them, eventually marrying Masayo some years later when Saya was nine, he was disowned by all the relatives and his friends from his first marriage. Saya didn't know the details, but she'd met hardly any of her stepfather's relatives.

'It's not that he doesn't have any, though,' her mother had said. 'You did meet Shoko a couple of times, you know.'

Shoko was her aunt's name. She hadn't got along at all well with the relatives, and was the only one who had been unperturbed by the scandal of her brother's separation and divorce. She even allowed Masayo and Yoichiro to visit her after he'd been disowned. Saya had absolutely no recollection of her.

'There's a photo somewhere.'

In the dog-eared photo that her mother produced, only Yoichiro and Masayo sat close together smiling, while Saya cuddled her soft toy rabbit and looked like she was about to cry. Aunt Shoko stood awkwardly to one side glaring stiffly into the lens like one of those farmers from a bygone era who feared their soul would be stolen by the camera.

Eventually they'd been defeated by Aunt Shoko's misanthropy and had stopped keeping in touch. Nevertheless, Shoko had made the effort to turn up to Yoichiro's funeral two years ago, and that was how Saya knew at least that she lived in the house in Yamanashi.

When Aunt Shoko died, her local city council had contacted Masayo and Saya. Since Shoko's brother had already passed away, she had specified in her will that her estate should go to Saya, as her brother's daughter. Given the circumstances, Saya and her mother had arranged a funeral for her. They had wanted to inform those who had known her, and found some contact details in the few letters they discovered in her house. In the end, two sets of distant relatives and three former colleagues from the credit union turned up.

It had been a lot of work to complete all the necessary procedures, collect Shoko's body from the hospital and arrange the funeral. Still, she was Yoichiro's sister and Masayo did everything she could. After some time had gone by, following Shoko's birthday in April she decided to move her ashes to the temple vault in Hachioji to be with Yoichiro's, and Saya had come here today to collect them.

Shoko's only sibling had been Yoichiro, so if she really had a nephew Saya could only think that he must be Yoichiro's child. The thought that this young man could be a son by Yoichiro's former wife did cross her mind, but as far as she knew he hadn't had any children from his first marriage. Plus he looked younger than she was. Noting her sceptical look, he relented and confessed.

'Well, not a blood relation, but kind of a nephew. He was like an uncle to me.'

'Uncle?' Saya sat bolt upright. 'There must be some mistake. Aunt Shoko was a woman.'

'But I'm not talking about Shoko,' he said, unperturbed. 'I'm talking about Yoshinobu, who used to live with her.'

'Yoshinobu?'

'He was like an uncle to me.'

'That's not what I mean. What has he got to do with Aunt Shoko?'

'I guess you could say he was Shoko's man.'

'Man?'

'Well, they were living together.'

'First I heard of it.'

'You can't believe that a woman past seventy could have a lover? I can. I saw them together, after all. They were about the same age and got along really well as a couple, you know. It was like they lived in a world of their own.'

He pointed to a bitter summer orange tree heavy with fruit in a corner of the garden. 'She used to boil things like that up to make jam, and the house always smelled great. At least, it did whenever I visited, once a year or so. She usually gave me some marmalade or plum jam to take home with me. There must be some jars left in their usual place in the kitchen.'

Saya hurried through to the kitchen, ripping open cupboard doors until she found one with a number of jars of homemade jam.

'So you were acquainted with Aunt Shoko,' she finally admitted.

He nodded, and introduced himself to her as Takashi Yamaji.

Yoshinobu had run his own local odd-jobs business, he told her.

'Odd-jobs?'

'Yep. He died about a year ago. I wasn't related to him by blood, but he had helped me a lot and I would always drop in to say hello whenever I was in the area.' He pointed at an old-fashioned black telephone placed in the hall outside the living room. 'The number for his business, Osako Odd Jobs, is stuck on that.'

Saya went out into the cool hallway and saw that the contact number for Osako Odd Jobs cut from the phone directory was visible beneath yellowing sellotape that was curling at the edges.

'Osako?'

'That's his name. Yoshinobu Osako.'

'And Mr Osako was in a relationship with my aunt?'

'He was living with her.'

'But I'd always heard that she wasn't at all sociable.'

'Maybe not with other people. They were both fairly well on in years, and were probably happy just to enjoy life together. They weren't the sort to have friends over, but I came here quite a few times, you know.'

'How long had they been living together?'

'Five years. No, it must have been about six years.'

'That long?'

'You never knew, even though you're her niece?'

Saya had the feeling he was reproaching her. For all that her aunt hadn't wanted company, it had never even occurred to her to worry about the old woman living out here alone.

'Well, I can't say I'm surprised,' Takashi Yamaji said lightly. 'I can kind of understand why they wouldn't have informed you. They weren't that type.'

Her aunt's house was deep in a desolate, abandoned farming area, and her nearest neighbour was almost a kilometre away. The bus stop was a couple of kilometres away. Saya had come from Tokyo by car and wondered how on earth her aunt had managed in a place like this without one.

'Was Mr Osako single?'

'He might have been married in the past. As far as I know, though, he was single. I wonder why they never married? Given their advanced age, I suppose they felt it was too much trouble. They must already have been in their late sixties by the time they got to know each other.'

'How did they meet?' Saya asked.

SHOKO HANAWA HAD LIVED ALONE ever since turning sixty. She grew all her own vegetables in her garden and rarely ate meat or fish. She only occasionally took the bus to go shopping for rice and other necessities, and had no qualms about living as a recluse. People had said she was crazy when she purchased the run-down house and plot of land in an isolated village that had long been abandoned by young people, and where there were fewer old people year by year. But it wasn't long before they stopped saying even that, and after a while nobody bothered themselves about where this eccentric single woman was or what she was doing.

She never called anyone for help when a light bulb needed changing, or when the hot water heater for the bath was malfunctioning. Even when she lost some roof tiles in a typhoon, she climbed out onto the roof to fix it herself. The only thing she was scared of was lighting:

nobody knew this, but day or night, if she heard thunder she would bury herself under some quilts, cover her ears, and stay put trembling until it had passed.

But then something happened that she wasn't able to fix by herself: pee started leaking down through the ceiling.

It was early autumn when she'd started hearing sounds coming from the ceiling. There were thuds like children playing around in the attic, and she'd feared there might be rats living up there. Still, she didn't want to call anyone in, so had kept the problem at bay with a fumigant bought from the pharmacy and by tapping the ceiling with a broom handle.

Eventually, however, a large stain formed on the ceiling and she was troubled by an unpleasant smell. When liquid started dripping down and she realised it was animal urine, she could stand it no longer.

She looked up businesses dealing with 'Pest and Vermin Extermination' in the telephone directory, and since phoning was too much trouble she sent a postcard to the nearest of them, Osako Odd Jobs.

When Yoshinobu arrived at the old house at the address on the postcard, he was met by an emaciated old lady with big, wide-open eyes, who avoided eye contact and spoke falteringly. He could hardly believe she was the person who had called on his services. 'She looked more like a skinny weasel than anything,' he'd said.

Having long been in the business, however, when she showed him the stain on the living room ceiling he knew immediately what the situation was: there must be a palm civet living up there.

'A civet?' Shoko had frowned fearfully. 'Not a rat?'

'It's bigger than a rat, and a bit of a nuisance. Still, the way to get rid of it is pretty much the same. First I'll have to find how it got in, chase it out, and block up the hole. Then there'll be a lot of excrement to clear out, but I can handle that for you too.'

Yoshinobu briskly put up ladders here and there and started inspecting inside the roof. He clearly was no amateur.

'There aren't any young. It's alone,' he said, patting the dust off his work clothes.

'It is?' Shoko replied, just a little less tense than she had been to begin with.

'Palm civets are considered pests, but they've been around since olden times and were even said to bring good fortune. They've also been demonised for coming down into villages to steal food, the poor things. There are good ones too, after all.'

'Good ones?'

'Yes,' Yoshinobu said, pointing at his name written in kanji on his business card. 'You see? The characters for my name can also be read *dai hakubishin – great palm civet*.' He roared with laughter, evidently proud of the joke, but Shoko didn't laugh.

After that, Yoshinobu went regularly to Shoko's house. He tried this way and that to chase the civet out of the roof, threatening it with loud firecrackers and smoking it out with fumigant, but the animal was well settled and refused to come out. As a last resort, Yoshinobu decided he would have to catch it, and set a trap baited with a ripe banana. He would be back in two or three days to check on it, he said.

Three days later, after running around on other business, Yoshinobu went back to the house in the late afternoon just as it was starting to drizzle with rain. He was on his way up to the roof to check on the trap while it was still light, when suddenly the sky darkened. A lightning bolt ripped through the sky and there was a tremendous clap of thunder, and then the rain pelted down with a roar.

The eyes of the trapped civet glittered as it circled frantically inside the cage, and it almost managed to bite Yoshinobu's gloved finger through the bars. But Yoshinobu was more startled by the sight of Shoko shaking like a leaf, doubled over face down on the living room floor with two cushions over her head.

He put the cage in a corner of the veranda, covered it with a black cloth, washed his hands and face in the bathroom, and went back to Shoko in the living room.

'I caught it, so no need to worry any more,' he told her, but Shoko stretched out one of her trembling hands, the other still holding the cushions in place, and grabbed his arm.

'As soon as the storm's over I'll pour you some tea, so stay a bit longer,' she said.

And so he did.

He sat down at her side, with her still clutching his arm. She was just like a small animal terrified of the sound of thunder, he thought. Once the storm died down, as promised she made him some tea with leaves she'd roasted herself in an earthenware pot. In place of the usual sweets served with tea, she put out some homemade bread thinly spread with marmalade she'd made with bitter oranges from her garden. Yoshinobu finished it all, commenting on how tasty everything was.

Outside it was still raining and already dark, long past dinnertime, and Shoko asked Yoshinobu if he wouldn't stay to dinner before going home.

And so he did.

Rice steamed with chestnuts harvested from a nearby tree on the mountainside; stewed edible wild greens; burdock root slithers sautéed in soy sauce and sugar; soup made with leeks, taros and carrots from her vegetable garden: Yoshinobu ate it all up, saying over and over how delicious it all was.

'Do you always eat so well?' he asked.

Shoko pretended she didn't understand his question.

Then she poured herself a glass of homemade plum wine. 'Please excuse me, but it's my custom to have a glass after dinner and I don't feel the meal's complete without it,' she said. Unable to join her in a drink because he was driving, Yoshinobu took just a sip to see what it tasted like and thought regretfully that next time he'd come without the car.

It was getting late and the civet was beginning to screech in its cage, so Yoshinobu finally hauled himself up.

Shoko watched him pick up the cage and place it on the back of his truck. 'What's going to happen to it?' she asked.

'It's hurt itself,' Yoshinobu said, avoiding the question. 'It must have wanted to get out so badly that it struggled and caught its front paw on something.'

Shoko went up to the cage and looked closely at the cowering animal. 'What's going to happen to it?'

Yoshinobu looked embarrassed and scratched the bridge of his nose. 'Well, I feel sorry for the poor thing, but it did get itself caught so it can't be helped. It'll be put down.'

Shoko's face instantly clouded over. 'But if it hadn't come to my house, it wouldn't have been caught.'

'Well, that's true, but it's not like it can just choose to settle in your house, is it? The fella thinks this is his home. You can't live here together, after all.'

Shoko thought a moment, then said in a small voice, 'Can we really not live together, I wonder?'

'But you called me up because it was a problem, didn't you?' he said in exasperation.

'That's not what I mean. Is it possible to keep it as a pet?'

'A palm civet?'

'Can they be kept as pets?'

'Are you serious?'

Shoko nodded.

Yoshinobu gaped at her. 'Well, it's not impossible. But if you keep it, then you have to keep it for life. You can't decide later to kick it out. That wouldn't be fair.'

'I think I'd like to keep it.'

'There are certain procedures you have to take, and you'll have to build a hutch for it. Are you absolutely sure you want to go through with this?'

'I think so.'

'Really?'

'Yes, really.'

And so it was decided. Yoshinobu would handle the procedures, take the civet to the vet, and build a hutch for it in the garden, which meant that he would be going to Shoko's house all the more frequently.

And at some point Yoshinobu stopped going back to his own home. He would leave Shoko's house for work, and afterwards go back there, feed the civet and in turn be fed by Shoko. Whenever the roof tiles were damaged in a typhoon, it became his job to fix them. Buying household necessities and rice from the grocery store two kilometres away also became his job. And so the couple lived together, caring for the palm civet.

Whether or not it was true that civets brought good fortune, happiness certainly came to Shoko and Yoshinobu along with their pet civet.

Potatoes, chestnuts, carrots, burdock roots, udo, Japanese pepper, edible wild greens, rape blossom, green onions, Chinese chives, wax gourds, plums, bitter oranges, loquats: Shoko grew everything in her garden. Yoshinobu picked wild mushrooms on the mountainside, and bought in fish and meat when he felt like eating them. Although Shoko never ate meat or fish on her own, she wasn't a vegetarian and would cook and eat whatever Yoshinobu brought home with him.

There is a legend about palm civets. Once upon a time, long ago when they were believed to be supernatural creatures that fell to earth with a lightning bolt, there was a maiden who fell in love with one. The village girls were skilled at drying ripe persimmons to make a tasty sweet snack, and one day a passing samurai beseeched one of them to give him one, so she did. The next day the handsome samurai came to thank her with some beautiful chrysanthemums, and informed her parents that he wanted her hand in marriage. Her father rejected him on the pretext of their difference in status, but eventually was worn down by the samurai's persistence and gave his permission. The samurai had her dress in travel attire, and together they left the village. They became a loving couple and it was said that, when they held each other all night long, joy ran through their bodies like a bolt of lightning. One night a few years later, lightning struck the plot of land where the couple lived, and two beautiful thunder beasts together rose up in the sky along the jagged light as it split the heavens. The villagers gossiped that the maiden had fallen in love with a thunder beast, and had turned into one herself and risen to heaven.

'A THUNDER BEAST?' asked Saya.

'That's right. It's a legendary creature that appears in old folk tales, but some believe it's actually a palm civet,' Takashi said, a mischievous grin on his handsome face.

It wasn't that Saya doubted what he was telling her about Shoko, but it was so utterly removed from what she knew of her aunt and the stories she'd heard about her that she didn't know what to think. She went again to the kitchen and found that there was indeed some deep amber homemade plum wine in large wide-mouthed jars.

Saya and Takashi Yamaji went out into the garden. In one corner there was a fenced-off area with a large hutch containing a low-growing tree and a tree hollow for nesting.

'Is this the hutch?' Saya asked.

He nodded. 'The civet's lifespan was shorter than your aunt's, but I think she cared for it for almost five years. Yoshinobu would come over regularly to teach her how to look after it, and would always stay for dinner. I suppose he started staying over so he could drink some plum wine too and eventually ended up living here.'

'But it's completely different from the image I had of my aunt. How can I put it ... she was a bit like a withered old tree, a spinster with nothing remotely sexy about her or any hint of having had any male friends.'

'A withered old tree?'

He was clearly offended, and Saya realised she'd said too much. All she knew of her aunt was that photo where she was glaring fiercely at the camera, and then more recently seeing her burn incense at her stepfather's funeral.

'A photo,' Saya said suddenly. 'Are there any photos of her? I really don't know much about her at all.'

'I doubt it. They weren't like that. They weren't the type to pose for the camera.'

No, I don't suppose they would have had their photos taken, Saya thought. She didn't know anything about them, but that much she could well believe.

'Oh, hang on,' he exclaimed, taking his mobile phone out of his pocket. 'There is one! I took it when I was over here once. Look!'

He held out his phone for her to see. There on the LCD screen was a photo of an animal with a stripe of white fur down its nose.

'Eh? But…' Saya stammered.

'Anything wrong?'

'It's an animal …'

'Yes, their pet civet, taken here. See? This is the cage, and this here is the tree.'

'My aunt and Mr Osako aren't in it, though.'

'I told you they weren't the type.'

On closer look, the civet in the photograph had its front paw bandaged. So it was true that her aunt had kept a pet civet.

'And none of them are still alive now, are they? Neither the civet, nor Mr Osako, nor my aunt,' Saya said, staring at the hutch.

'It's true, they've all passed away.' Takashi Yamaji took a packet of cigarettes out of his trouser pocket. 'Do you mind?' he asked, before lighting up. His smoke wafted skywards.

'And so, Mr Yamaji, what brought you here today?'

'I just happened to be passing and saw the car, so

thought someone must be here. I was hoping to be allowed to light an incense stick for your aunt.'

'There isn't a family altar, just the urn. It wasn't a religious funeral.'

'It doesn't matter, I can just pay my respects to the urn. It's the sentiment that counts, that's all.'

He held his palms together in prayer before the white urn and remained there for a while with his head bowed.

'Where's Mr Osako's grave? Is it near here?' Saya asked him as he sat with his eyes closed.

After a while, he opened them. 'No, it's a long way away. Quite a bit further up. He was a bit of a wanderer, that one.'

Saya tilted her head enquiringly. By 'further up', did he mean 'further north'?

'It wouldn't have made any difference to him whether he had a grave or not. He wasn't interested in things like that,' Takashi Yamaji said bluntly.

Saya began to feel that things were falling into place in her mind. Maybe her aunt really had had a lover. If so, he must have been a bit eccentric too. She could imagine two people like that being able to live together.

'Oh, but if you're interested, I do know where the civet is buried,' Takashi Yamaji said.

'The civet?'

'The civet died before Yoshinobu, and he buried it beneath an akebi tree on the mountainside behind the house.'

'You mean the civet has a grave?'

'Yep.'

'Is it far?'

'No, not at all. About ten minutes by car.'

THE MAIN REASON Saya had Takashi Yamaji guide her to the civet's final resting place was because he'd told her, 'I'm pretty sure those two didn't have any interest in what happens after death, but I'm not as pragmatic as they were. I kind of have the feeling that they met up somewhere after they died. Like, for example, near where the civet is at rest.'

In the car on the way up the mountain, Saya began feeling a little heady. The good-looking, muscular young man in the passenger seat beside her smelled sweet, like ripe fruit or aromatic berries.

They got out of the car and walked along a mountain path. Every time she stumbled in the undergrowth, Takashi Yamaji reached out a suntanned arm to steady her.

After a while, he pointed to a tree with a vine-like stem and purple flowers. Up close, she could see that alongside the big purple flowers there were other smaller white flowers with a pink centre.

'There are two types of flowers?'

He looked amused at her surprise. 'Haven't you ever seen akebi flowers? These large ones are female, and the numerous small white ones are male.'

'So is this is the civet's grave?'

'That's right. Apparently Yoshinobu was fond of akebi fruits, and when they were in season Shoko would come and pick them and use them in cooking. Although they're sweet and tasty just as they are.' He smiled at her.

Saya stood before the akebi flowers and put her palms together. It was a mild sunny day, and some petals from the mountain cherry blossoms fluttered down around them in the gentle breeze.

Even now Saya didn't quite know why things turned out the way they did. However, in the car on the way back to her aunt's house with this man who smelled of sweet fruit and berries, and as they sat chatting on the veranda in the westering sun, she felt her body growing hot. Eventually she caught his arm and pulled him to her.

He regarded her with his large round dark eyes for a while, then smiled as though he understood everything and covered her lips with his own.

It wasn't he who led, but Saya. Running her tongue slowly along his neck, she drew his large hand to her breast. Softly he teased her nipple. It instantly stiffened, and a sigh escaped her. A warm, frothy sensation rose gradually from her groin.

Little by little his lips moved downwards and caught her nipple, and his fingers caressed her between her legs, where she was hot and wet. A tingling sensation ran through her.

Unable to wait any longer, she pushed his fingers away, and held his hips as he thrust deep inside her. Warm liquid spurted into her and a flash of pleasure ran from her groin up her back, through her shoulder blades up to the top of her head, making her head swim. She arched her back to stop that feeling of bliss from leaving, as if to retain it in her body just that little bit longer.

And that was how they passed the evening.

After getting dressed, Saya was gripped by an unaccountable sensation. She was utterly contented and didn't feel in the slightest guilty, she realised in surprise.

'I–It's not like I do this sort of thing all the time,' she stammered.

Takashi Yamaji nodded quietly. He was sitting on the veranda gazing at the bitter orange tree in the garden, the same as when he had arrived.

'I'm involved with someone in Tokyo – ' she started, but before she could finish he turned to face her and shook his head.

'But I ... just now ... it felt so...' Good, she was going to say, but her words trailed off.

'For me too, even more so,' he said, and turned his gaze back to the garden.

After a few moments he got up to leave.

She saw him off as far as the gate. As she waved goodbye, she suddenly felt another flash run through her body and a slight breath escaped her.

After he'd gone, Saya tried calling the number for Osako Odd Jobs, but connected only with a recorded message saying that the number was no longer in use.

She would return to Tokyo with her aunt's ashes, and the next time she came here would be to dispose of the property, she thought. She started looking in drawers wondering if she might find some keepsake from the time her aunt had lived with her lover.

What she found was an album full of photos of the palm civet. Its round eyes resembled those of the young man who had just left, she realised.

Saya only ever met Takashi Yamaji that one time.

Back in Tokyo, she told her mother Masayo, 'It seems Aunt Shoko kept a palm civet as a pet.'

Sometime after they'd laid Shoko's ashes to rest, Saya began wondering whether the story of her aunt having had a lover was really true or not. Maybe she'd simply seen out her last years caring for the civet.

As more time went by, she began to have the feeling that Yoshinobu hadn't been a man after all, but the civet itself.

And, as the years passed, she began to think that maybe everything that happened that day had actually been a dream.

Childhood Friends

THAT'S RIGHT, I'M CLOSING DOWN THIS BAR. At the end of the month.

Yeah, a long time – twenty years. Not one good memory to show for it either. Worked myself to the bone and business has just gone downhill the whole time. But what's a girl to do?

I tell you, I'm sick and tired of it. I mean, look at my poor finger!

Two nights ago ... I was heading home after closing up when some weirdo starts following me. Lots of them around here. Damn weirdos.

I told him to get lost and started running. I know, in these heels! Can you believe it? But he was persistent, I'll give him that. Grabbed me by the arm and twisted my finger. Yeah, twisted it. Right there. Typical. Some guys think if they rough you up a bit, you'll give in. But I managed to get away.

I'd been drinking, of course. It's part of the job, right? Don't know if that's why, but by the time I got home my finger was ginormous! No, it didn't hurt a bit; alcohol's a great painkiller. But it was a nasty shock.

Damn weirdos. That's what I hate about this job. I've had it up to here.

Still, I've got to work, don't I? The bar's not going to run itself.

So I go to the doctor's and show them my ginormous finger. They hand me a prescription and I'm, like, is all this really necessary? What's happening these days? You'd think they were giving out candy. Every time I eat, I've got to swallow a dozen pills. Seriously! Want to see?

There, like I said ... well, maybe not a dozen but close enough. I mean, how do they expect me to swallow all this?

Then last night one of my regulars comes in to say goodbye and I end up drinking like four shots of tequila in a row. All of a sudden, I start feeling queasy and my heart's racing.

Yeah, exactly, 'cos of the pills.

You know me. Normally I can knock back four shots of tequila without batting an eyelid, right? I mean, you have to be able to hold your drink in this line of work.

But last night I felt all light-headed and the room was spinning – like I was high or something. Fortunately, my customer puts two and two together and says it must be the pills. So I stop drinking and go and lie down over there. Yeah, right on that sofa. Anyway, that's why I'm only drinking oolong tea tonight. Sorry 'bout that ...

Sure, I'm sad about closing this place. But business is awful.

I mean, hardly anyone drinks Dom Pérignon these days. But I have to stock it just in case. There's a lot of stuff like that. This bar eats money. Not to mention it's getting old and repairs don't come cheap. Costs a fortune to run this place.

What am I going to do? After this, you mean? That's the big question, isn't it? You really want to know? All right ... I'm getting married.

Hey, don't look so surprised! How old am I? Don't you know better than to ask a girl her age? Okay, forty-eight. Yeah, four eight. Why, how old do I look?

Why shouldn't I? I mean, *he* popped the question. Now stop it, you're embarrassing me. I'm too sober to talk about it. Really, not without a few drinks. How about a highball? Oh, the pills? Never mind them. Don't worry, I'll make it weak ...

Yeah, I mean it. I'm getting married.

No, he's not a customer. Not even a former one. In fact, he's never set foot in here.

Who is he? Let's see, where should I begin?

Well, he used to work for an NGO overseas. Spent most of his life in South-East Asia. These past five years he's been working on the Thai–Burmese border. Before that he was in Laos – or was it Cambodia? Anyway, I know he spent a long time in Cambodia. No, never been there myself. I went to Thailand once hoping to meet him in Bangkok, but somehow the timing didn't work out. But now he's come back to Japan. For good.

So we've always had a long-distance relationship.

How long is 'always'? You do ask an awful lot of questions! Well, at times it's felt like we were a million light years apart, emotionally speaking. We only became close again about two years ago. One day I stumbled across his profile on Facebook. I wasn't sure it was him at first, but I sent him a message and sure enough it was. Incredible, right? Life's funny that way. It's a whole new world now. Yeah, good ol' Facebook!

The thing is, you see, we were childhood friends. Known each other since we were twelve; went to middle school and high school together ...

What's so funny? Stop it! It's romantic! Don't laugh!

Yeah, like a dream come true. Hey, remember 'The Tide is High'? No, it's not a movie; it's a song. By Blondie. No, that's the name of the group. How can you not know it? It's got this groovy reggae beat ... It was even in a beer commercial recently. Anyway, it's like that ... just like that. Every time I hear it, the past thirty years slip away. I'm back in high school; it's the autumn of our second year. A wave's rising inside me, swallowing me up, but I'm holding on, as the song says. And I'm going to be his number one!

I know, I'm no good at telling stories – not coherently anyway. But you knew that. All I'm saying is, that song is special to me. It's the song we first danced to together back in high school. And now I'm going to marry him!

If anyone can tell that story coherently, I'd like to hear it!

—

SHUHEI'S FLIGHT LANDED at Tokyo's Haneda Airport shortly past noon. He'd never been in the newly completed international terminal before and he probably wouldn't be coming back anytime soon, seeing as this wasn't another short-term visit. It was a weekday and the neat little airport was nearly deserted but for the odd tour group being shepherded along by a guide.

As he emerged from customs into the arrivals hall, dragging his big suitcase behind him, Rey, excitedly waving her hands in the air, rushed over to greet him with a huge smile on her face.

As Shuhei still stood gaping at his unfamiliar surroundings, she took his suitcase over to the baggage delivery service counter and quickly filled in the delivery slip. In no time she was back.

'Hey, did you know? This place has become quite the tourist attraction. I hear there's a bunch of nice souvenir shops upstairs – shall we take a peek?' said Rey, pulling Shuhei by the hand.

In high spirits, Rey began browsing the shops, their store fronts hung with rows of old-fashioned paper lanterns.

'That handkerchief is pretty, isn't it? Now that's simply adorable. Oh my, just look at the price! Check out this tote bag – what were they thinking? This is to die for! I wouldn't mind that, either. How about this? Come take a look at these, Shu. Oh, I just adore smartphone cases; I've got a collection at home. You can never have too many!'

That day Rey's shoulder-length hair was loose, with just the part in front tied back so it didn't fall over her forehead. Watching her as she strolled amongst the souvenir shops, intently perusing the merchandise,

Shuhei was reminded of being at a festival market. Something about the newly constructed airport shopping area evoked the temporary wooden stalls vendors set up outside temples and shrines on festival days. He recalled attending such a festival at a Shinto shrine, late one summer in his youth, with a girl he'd had a crush on – not Rey, of course, but a classmate of his from primary school. An image suddenly came back to him of buying her a balloon and a yo-yo with his pocket money, of her frolicking gaily about in her colourful cotton kimono. It had been his first date.

Shuhei picked up a handkerchief with a pattern of little old-fashioned locomotives. Rey had eyed it covetously for a while before finally saying it was too expensive. She was now engrossed in examining some garish character merchandise and didn't notice as he headed over to the cashier with it.

It had been roughly a week since Shuhei had left the tiny Thai village where he'd been living. After changing buses several times, he'd at last arrived in Bangkok, stayed several days at a friend's house, then flown on to Hong Kong. He spent two more nights there on his own before boarding a flight back to Japan. It hadn't been the quickest or most efficient route home, but after living so many years abroad, Shuhei was perhaps somewhat ambivalent about returning permanently to Japan. A quarter of a century had passed since he'd dropped out of university in his early twenties and gone off to Bangladesh, where he got a job with a local NGO. For a very long time, he thought he might never return to Japan.

His father's sudden death at the beginning of the year had changed all that. Shuhei had returned to Tokyo at once upon receiving the news. Since his mother's death, his father had lived alone in the old house where Shuhei grew up. He'd kept away all these years believing he and his father had nothing to talk about, but suddenly he regretted his long absence. Having lived outside of Japan for so long, he could only stand by helplessly, not knowing what to do, as the neighbourhood association took care of the arrangements for his father's funeral. 'Your dad told me you work overseas helping people in developing countries,' said one elderly gentleman, who appeared to be overseeing things. Then he added pointedly: 'He could have used a bit of help too, you know.'

At his father's wake Shuhei had seen Rey, a classmate from middle and high school, for the first time in thirty years, when she appeared dressed in mourning to offer a stick of incense at the altar. Two years ago, they had reconnected by chance over Facebook and rekindled their old friendship. Over the course of exchanging messages, Rey had opened up to him about her life. He'd heard rumours from other classmates, too, so he hadn't been unprepared. Still, he was taken aback by Rey's transformation. Her long hair was tied up in a neat bun and she wore a black two-piece outfit with black stockings and black high heels.

Two days later, the day after the cremation and burial, Shuhei saw Rey again.

They had arranged to meet in Shibuya, which in the old days they had both had to pass through on their way to and from school. Shuhei was astonished to see how much the area around the station had changed; all the places he remembered were gone: his favourite bookstore, record store, even the Gotoh Planetarium.

'I hear they've built a new one,' said Rey matter-of-factly.

'A new what?'

'Planetarium, silly. Where would Shibuya be without one?'

They went to a bar on Dogenzaka; after several drinks, one thing led to another and they ended up at a nearby hotel. So much time had passed that Shuhei had trouble connecting the Rey he saw before him now with the Rey he'd known in high school. If he'd tried to reason it out, he probably wouldn't have been able to do what he did. But in reality, it wasn't so difficult. Shuhei kissed Rey's full, rounded breasts, then she took his cock in her mouth, slowly enveloping and caressing it with her tongue, gently at first, then stronger and faster until her tongue was racing around so busily it felt she must have two or three.

When they were done, they lay on the bed watching TV, Rey's head resting on Shuhei's arm. Some sort of talk show was on, featuring a panel of celebrities, but Shuhei didn't recognise any of them. Rey dozed off and began snoring gently.

Later, when Shuhei returned to Thailand, Rey came to Narita airport to see him off. 'Take care,' she said, throwing her arms around his neck. She didn't ask when he would be back. Instead, she just kept waving the whole time he stood in line at immigration, right up until he was out sight.

Indeed, until six months ago, Shuhei had had no intention of returning to Japan permanently. When he said, 'See you later' and waved goodbye to Rey, he imagined they'd simply settle back into their well-worn daily routines, checking in with each other from time to time on Facebook.

But it was not to be.

When financial difficulties suddenly forced Shuhei's NGO to close the office where he'd been working, his boss had approached him about transferring to Tokyo. 'I'd go myself except I've got a family here,' said the man, who was married to a Thai woman and had three young children; he even looked like one of the locals, so much time had he spent under the tropical sun. 'But there's nothing to prevent you from going, is there?'

Tokyo? For a moment, Shuhei had been unable to process the word. He still had the house his father had left him, for he had no siblings and the inheritance taxes had been negligible. But it was quite old; he'd been planning to have it torn down and to sell off the lot. The option of returning to Japan and living there had arisen only because of his job – or had it?

He could refuse, of course, and ask to be transferred somewhere else in Asia instead, or even to Europe, where his NGO also had offices, though whether such a request would be granted was another matter.

In the end, Shuhei wasn't quite sure what made him decide to return to Tokyo: his job situation, his father's empty house or his advancing years. It felt as though it was all these things and yet none of them.

When the option of returning to Japan for good first crossed his mind, Shuhei had suddenly pictured Rey's face – or, rather, Rey's Facebook profile picture, with half her face hidden by her long hair. Since returning to Thailand, whenever Shuhei happened to be in the office in the early afternoon, he would check his computer for the little circle with Rey's profile picture that indicated whether she was online. Then they'd trade innocuous messages or sometimes live chat about places they'd been together long ago, movies they'd seen recently, and other trivialities.

I'm thinking of returning to Japan ...

It occurred to Shuhei there was no one other than Rey to whom he could say this. He didn't know anyone else in Japan. Now his father was dead, there was no one besides Rey linking him to his past: to his twenty-year-old self, before he set off to wander Asia; to his teenage self, dancing with her for the first time; and even to his younger self, living in that old house with his parents, going fishing in Tokyo Bay with his father, or heart pounding with the thrill of asking a girl out on a date for the first time. There was no one to connect him to those times, apart from—

'Rey?'

Shuhei's reminiscences were interrupted by his own voice. He looked around and found Rey still scouring the shelves of souvenirs.

'Yes?' she answered, looking up at him. In her small, neat features, Shuhei could clearly discern the Rey of their teenage years. As he mentally photoshopped Rey's face, stripping away the freckles, the tiny crow's feet, reversed what was no doubt the work of the plastic surgeon's knife, there was no mistaking the face of his old friend.

Shuhei unceremoniously held out a small paper bag containing the handkerchief he'd just bought for her. 'Sorry, I completely forgot to bring you anything from Thailand ...' he mumbled.

To his surprise, Rey blushed. 'Thank you, Shu,' she said quietly, shyly caressing his outstretched forearm with her index finger; then she added: 'Say, how about going to the planetarium?'

'Where?'

'Here in the airport; there's a small one.' She grabbed his arm. 'It's just over there. C'mon, the show should be about to start.'

Rey led Shuhei over to the entrance to a café. Sure enough, a small crowd was gathered outside, apparently awaiting the start of the next show.

Soon the doors opened and they all filed into a small dome-shaped theatre and sat down on hard chairs arrayed around the sides of the still brightly lit room. Staring up at the ceiling, Shuhei mused that, six months ago, when he and Rey had met in Shibuya, he'd learned his old planetarium was gone; now here he was in a new one, within minutes of landing at this unfamiliar airport, after returning from abroad.

Long ago – from sometime in primary school to about halfway through middle school – Shuhei's dream had been to become an astronomer. At one time it had felt as though he practically lived at the Gotoh Planetarium in Shibuya; he'd seen all the shows umpteen times. How many weekday afternoons had he sat there in the dark in his school uniform, looking up at the starry man-made sky overhead? The planetarium had felt enormous, no doubt partly because he'd been small. Compared to the planetarium of his childhood memories, this one he was in now seemed like a toy. As son cubano or some such Latin-sounding music streamed through the speakers on the walls, the seats quickly filled up and the lights were slowly dimmed.

'Starting in late June in the northern hemisphere,' a recorded narrator began, 'three bright stars forming a triangle become visible in the eastern sky. These are Vega, located in the constellation of Lyra; Deneb, in the constellation of Cygnus; and Altair, in the constellation of Aquila. Together these stars make up what is called the Summer Triangle, which shines brightly through the night and has, since ancient times, served to guide travellers...'

As Shuhei listened absent-mindedly to this familiar-sounding commentary, he became aware of the sound of quiet and regular breathing, and then Rey's body slowly slumped against his. He reached over and gently put his hand on her head until it came to rest on his shoulder. A faint smile rose to his lips. How typical of his old friend to fall asleep the moment the lights were turned out! No doubt Rey had been up until nearly dawn, closing up the small bar she had run all by herself for twenty years. Despite his telling her there was no need to come to the airport, she'd insisted on being there to greet him. Normally, she'd probably have been at home fast asleep, and remained so until the evening, when she got ready to go out to the bar again.

'Let us now turn our gaze to the southern sky ... The biggest and brightest star one sees is called Antares, in the constellation of Scorpius. And do you see that ladle-shaped cluster of six stars, which looks like a small version of the Big Dipper? That is known as the Milk Dipper ...'

He and Rey were the same age, Shuhei thought to himself as his old friend snored peacefully beside him; the passage of time was the same for her as it was for him. While he had been traipsing around Asia's hinterlands from dawn to dusk, day in and day out, year after year, helping farmers to grow better crops and establish fair-trade cooperatives, Rey had been running her bar all by herself and diligently saving her money. Then she'd had her operation. Shuhei didn't know whether it was because of the surgery, the hormones she was taking or simply genetics, but even after all these years her skin was still smooth and taut and she looked far younger than he did.

It was a short programme, just fifteen minutes, and seemed to end in no time. As the summer sky gradually brightened, a vaguely Caribbean-sounding melody streamed in over the speakers.

Beside him, Rey stirred and gave a big yawn.

'Sleep well?'

At this gentle jibe, Rey pouted and jerked her chin away in feigned petulance. Then something suddenly caused her to turn to him and smile.

'Hey, remember this song?'

Rey held up an index finger and waved her hand in rhythm to the music. Soon her shoulders were swaying back and forth, and, as they made their way towards the exit, she began singing along to the song.

When Shuhei still gave no sign of recognition, Rey sighed and whispered in his ear: 'Our second year of high school – the last night of the festival …'

At last, Shuhei realised what she was talking about. He nodded his head several times.

Every October their school held its annual festival. On the closing night, all the parents and other guests, including the students from the local girls' school, were kicked out, and the boys held a big party. That year it took place in the schoolyard; there were fireworks, some student bands played, people danced, and it turned into a sort of wild party. That was the first time Shuhei had seen Rey dressed as a girl.

At the time, though, no one suspected what Rey was going through emotionally. The annual party was a chance for the students to let down their hair; quite a few had shown up in drag and all manner of bizarre attire. And now Shuhei remembered: the song playing when he saw Rey that night was Blondie's 'The Tide is High'.

It hadn't been a big school – everyone pretty much knew everyone else, by name at least. Still, up until that point Rey and Shuhei had barely spoken to each other. But that night, for some reason, they had danced together over and over. From then on, they would often talk about movies and music, or what they planned to do when they graduated.

'Come to think of it, that's when it all started, wasn't it?' said Shuhei. 'Our friendship.'

Rey's eyes crinkled at the corners as she quietly smiled.

—

YOU HAVE TO PROMISE not to repeat this. I've never told anyone ...

The first time I set eyes on him was our first day of middle school. You know how there's an opening ceremony at the beginning of the year, and you all line up in the auditorium according to classroom and have to listen to speeches? Well, he was in the classroom right next to mine.

It was love at first sight, I tell you, love at first sight. What's it been now – thirty-five years? Sorry, I must sound like a broken record ... But who'd have thought it'd take that long to consummate my first love? And at forty-eight! Talk about fate.

Of course, we were just middle-schoolers. He probably barely knew I existed. I'd gaze at him longingly on the train to and from school. We had to change train lines in Shibuya, and he'd usually stop at the planetarium on his way home ... Well, I suppose he liked gazing at the stars. People said he wanted to be an astronomer when he grew up ... Anyway, I'd secretly follow him inside.

What's wrong with that? Him? I don't think he ever had a clue. He's a bit thick when it comes to things like that. But that's what I love about him. Don't you think it's nice just to admire someone from afar sometimes? What if I'd bumped into him there? I suppose I'd have said something like, 'I come here all the time 'cos I want to be an astronomer when I grow up – how 'bout you?' and we could have bonded over that. I even bought a bunch of books on astronomy and boned up on constellations and stuff. Talk about boring! But I didn't have the balls to go up and talk to him, and he never noticed me. In the end, even he seemed to tire of the planetarium, and so I stopped going. Basically, that was middle school for me.

Once I spotted him in Shibuya out on a date with a girl. We must have been about thirteen then. I think she was a classmate of his from primary school. It was a weekend, so I assumed they'd gone to a movie or something. Did it break my heart? Yeah, I suppose, but it's not like I hadn't expected it. Still, I was pretty depressed for a while.

In October our school held its annual festival, with a big party for all the students on the final night. A few teachers stuck around to keep an eye on things, but parents and outsiders weren't allowed in. Our school had quite a bohemian reputation and things could get pretty rowdy.

That was where I finally got to dance with him. It was our second year in high school. We even held hands. This was the early-eighties, remember, so when I say we danced, it was like, 'It's disco time!' Not that stuff they play in clubs these days. Good ol' fashioned disco. Such as? Oh, music you've probably never heard of: The Nolans, Arabesque, and that one-hit wonder Dschinghis Khan.

But the first song we danced to was 'The Tide is High'. It's got this kind of slow beat, right? I mean, it just ... How can I put it? It perfectly captured how I felt at that moment, especially the bit about not being the kind of girl who gives up! It just spoke to me, know what I mean? The second verse always makes me cry: where she's singing about all the girls wanting him to be their man but she's going to wait her turn ... of course, I never thought I'd have to wait three decades! Not that I was literally waiting all that time ...

Last month he returned home from Thailand for good. I went to meet him at the airport. Haneda's new international terminal. Have you been? They've even got a planetarium there. We weren't in a hurry or anything, so we went in – for old times' sake. And guess what? They played it ... our song! You get it, right? It had to be a sign. I couldn't get it out of my head after that ... What do they call it these days – an 'ear worm'? And I thought to myself, *Dammit, I'm not the sort of girl who gives up either!*

Anyway, about a week later, he calls and says we should live together – his idea, not mine. He said his house is old but it's too big for one person.

Sure, I was surprised. 'Why all of a sudden?' I asked him. And he said: 'I've just been thinking – about the rest of my life. And I want to spend it with you.'

So I'm closing the bar at the end of the month.

Yeah, a long time – twenty years. Not one good memory to show for it either. Worked myself to the bone and business has just gone downhill the whole time.

When I told him I was tired of running the bar, he said, 'Then stop. Close it. You don't have to do this to yourself any more. I'm here now.'

That knocked me for a loop. No one's ever said anything like that to me before. Never even occurred to me someone might.

It just goes to show, if you live long enough ...

Of course, I'm only forty-eight. If we're lucky we've got thirty more years together.

Well, thank you! It's so kind of you to say that. I hope we'll be very happy too. Could you pass me a tissue? Just over there ... thanks.

I love the word *marriage*, don't you? It just has a beautiful ring to it.

I'll move my stuff in once he's done clearing out the house, then we'll start our life together. I've already filled in the marriage licence. That's right, I officially changed my gender, what ... five years ago now?

No, I never thought I'd see this day, not in a million years.

An impossible dream ... Yes, that's exactly what it seemed.

So that's why I'm in such a good mood tonight.

Sorry if I keep repeating myself. I'm just so happy.

Truly, blissfully happy.

The Harajuku House

THE GHOST STORY that has made the biggest impression on me so far was the one I heard at a gathering of college friends for a drinking party that went on late into the night. At one point a rather taciturn older man, greying at the temples, got up to speak. He was the manager of a small machine parts factory in Oita, Kyushu, in Tokyo on a business trip, and staying the night in my friend's house where the party was held. I'll call him W.

'I don't really believe in ghosts and stuff,' he said by way of starting. 'But it's possible I may actually have met one. I don't really like to call her that, though.'

—

IN THE LONG SPRING BREAK, after completing his first year of university, W had taken on a part-time job at an estate agent's upon the recommendation of a senior student. This was in the mid-1980s. He was handed a map of a section of Harajuku, and was to go door-to-door around the neighbourhood conducting a survey. It was probably a preliminary investigation for a property developer or some such thing, but that was not W's concern.

Map in hand, he turned off the busy tree-lined Omotesando into the backstreets where he normally never went, and suddenly found himself in the hush of a residential neighbourhood. Even now, once you step away from the popular shopping streets of Takeshita-dori and Omotesando, Harajuku is a separate world where people go about their daily lives.

It was a cold day, so to keep warm W walked quickly up the gentle slope. The house he was looking for was shielded by a concrete wall, at one end of which there was a sombre entrance like a sullenly open mouth. As he went through it, the temperature seemed to drop even further. In the garden, a large windmill palm spread its leaves like a gatekeeper concealing the house that lay beyond, so that the elegant residence was inconspicuous and retained a solitary air. W kept his eyes on the path, taking care not to stumble on the uneven paving stones, but looked up in surprise when, just in front of him, an azure-winged magpie suddenly flapped its wings and flew away. As he did so, the large house that he hadn't seen from outside loomed up before him. It was a striking presence, even for this residential district where there were many fine mansions. The left wing was entirely Western in style, with an imposing entrance and a roof that from afar looked grey but was actually the verdigris of copper sheet. The lower floor exterior was finished in scratched-face ceramic tiles, while the upper floor was coated in mortar and had three arched latticed windows with canopies.

To the right of this, connected by an enclosed corridor, was the Japanese-style wing with a veranda, shaded by trees, that overlooked the garden with a pond and stone lanterns. The shutters were not fully closed, and although at first glance it didn't look as though anybody was in, it would have been careless to go out leaving them like that.

Beside the front door of the Western-style building was a nameplate reading *Kimoto*. A grey cable ran from a circular black doorbell with a white knob at the centre, but given how old it looked W wondered whether it was even connected to the electricity and would ring or not. He was just about to ring it anyway when he felt the presence of someone behind him.

He turned to see a girl of about ten standing there. Her jet-black hair was cut in a short bob, with her fringe cut straight across above her eyebrows, and she was wearing a navy blue long, narrow dress that puffed out slightly over her arms, with white socks and patent leather shoes with a strap. It was a Sunday-best style of clothing that you rarely saw these days.

'Hello,' W said. 'Is this your house?'

The girl glared at him without answering.

'Is your mummy home?'

This time she quietly shook her head.

'So you're here on your own?'

She shook her head angrily.

'Where is everyone?'

'Not here.'

'Have they gone out somewhere?'

'No. Just, they aren't here,' she said, then ran off towards the back of the house.

W was left standing there by the front door feeling bewildered. She might be young, but surely she was old enough to answer him properly, he thought.

He pulled himself together and pressed the doorbell. As luck would have it, he heard a buzzer sound inside the house. He waited for ten seconds, then pressed it a second time. Nobody came to the door.

He tried the doorknob just in case, but it didn't turn. He gave up and went around to the veranda and reached through the half-open storm shutter to open the glass door, but this too was locked and just rattled as he shook it.

The little girl had been wearing her best clothes, so perhaps the family had just come back from a day out together, he thought. The parents might have remembered some shopping they needed to do and left the child here while they nipped out to get it. He wondered whether he should wait for them to come back, and looked at his watch. Better to come back another time. He still needed to visit a few more houses in order to meet his work quota for the day.

IT WAS A CHILLY DAY AGAIN when W next visited the house.

Before pressing the doorbell, he went into the garden to peep in at the veranda, and saw that this time the storm shutters were wide open. He slid the glass door open, and called out, 'Is anyone at home?'

After a few moments there was a quiet patter of footsteps along the corridor, then a curtain swished shut before his nose.

'Come to the front door,' he heard a woman's voice say.

W had grown up in the countryside where visitors generally felt more comfortable going to the veranda than to the front door, but it appeared that the custom was different in Tokyo. She must think he was rude, he thought with dismay.

He repressed an urge to run away and went back around to the front door, but then he worried about having come out dressed so casually in an old sweater and jeans. Hastily he searched for the business cards the office had provided him with to conduct the survey, then stood before a fuzzy reflection of himself in a decorative pane of glass in the door, and smoothed his hair with his hands a few times before pushing the doorbell.

It was taking an inordinate amount of time for the woman to come to the door. W stood there not knowing what to do, wondering whether she had decided not to answer, or perhaps hadn't heard the bell. Maybe he should ring it again. He was just about to give up and leave, when the door opened. Their eyes met.

She was surprisingly young. She wore a pale yellow cardigan over a round-collared blouse and a moss green skirt. The eyes looking – almost glaring – up at him were attractively large, and her lips were full. These parted, and she asked, 'Who are you?'

W was transfixed, unable to move.

The door quietly began to close, so he hastily pulled it open again. 'Wait!'

He wrenched it so hard that the woman, still holding onto the doorknob, lost her balance. She came flying out, arms outstretched, and caught hold of W's sweater with white fingers. Her eyebrows drew together as she glared up at him, and once again those full lips parted and she snapped 'Stop that!' at almost the same moment as he blurted out 'I'm sorry!'

She pulled herself upright. This time she didn't try to close the door, but stood there with her arms folded beneath her breasts as though to say, *if you have something to say then get on and say it.*

'Here,' he said, holding out his business card.

He was still a student and didn't yet know that the correct way to present someone with his business card was to hold it in both hands for them to accept, and he simply held it up for her to read as though he were a police officer showing his badge. She unfolded her arms, reached out a hand, took the card and looked at it.

'I'm going around houses in this neighbourhood conducting a survey. I just need to ask a few questions so if you don't have time now, I can leave the questionnaire with you and come pick it up from you later. I do hope you will fill it in for me.'

She stood for some moments chewing her lower lip and suspiciously staring first at the young man and then at his business card. Then she sighed and held out her hand.

'Huh?' He tensed, unsure what she meant, and once again she reached out and took the questionnaire between her index and middle finger. Plucking it smoothly out of W's hand, she said, 'I'll fill it in.'

The door closed.

He couldn't summon the nerve to ring the doorbell again, and anyway, she had at least taken the questionnaire from him. He would let an appropriate amount of time pass and then come back to collect it from her, he decided as he left.

The thought that he would return cheered him up, W told us. There was a spring in his step as he walked along the tree-lined avenue back to the station. This was long before anyone had even thought about pulling down Omotesando's iconic pre-war concrete apartment block and replacing it with a high-end shopping complex.

THE SMELL OF A CAKE baking emanated from the house.

This was the day when W set foot inside the residence for the first time. As he turned left off Omotesando and walked along the lane, the wall around the house looked even gloomier than the first time he'd seen it, but as he went into the garden he caught the sweet aroma of sugar and butter cooking.

This time he'd paid a little more attention to his appearance, and unusually for him was wearing a tie. The young woman's age was unclear, but W guessed she must be either about the same age as him or a little older. She had worn a hairband in her wavy shoulder-length hair, and her make-up had appeared quite mature compared to the female students he saw at university.

He smoothed down his hair, then rang the doorbell. Hearing her answer, he was relieved that she didn't sound angry. She opened the door. She was shorter than he was, and looking down at her he could see her white breasts peeping through the front of her blouse.

He'd assumed she would return the questionnaire to him at the front door, but she told him brightly to come in. 'It's too much bother to write it all down. Didn't you say you could ask me the questions?'

W noticed that she seemed in rather high spirits, he told us.

He took off his shoes and went inside. The place was spotlessly clean, and the corridor floor beneath the embroidered slippers put out for him had been polished to a shine. He was shown into the drawing room where a huge sofa as big as a bed and an armchair large enough to hold three children faced each other across an oval coffee table. The fireplace wasn't lit, but there were traces of fresh ash in it.

'Try some,' she said as he sat in the armchair curiously surveying his surroundings.

Placed in front of him was a gold-rimmed teacup and saucer, and a clearly expensive plate upon which was a pie with what looked like a soft custard filling. He realised that she must have made it that morning, enveloping the garden in that sweet aroma.

He did as he was told and took a bite, then grimaced slightly.

'Sweet, is it?' she asked him with a mischievous smile. Picking up the pie on her own plate between thumb and forefinger, she shamelessly opened her mouth and bit off about two-thirds.

'Mmm, it's sooooo sweet! Delicious!'

The filling was so cloying it was like eating sugar syrup. He nodded and smiled at her, and resolved to eat every last awful crumb. Having forced it all down, W took out the questionnaire. If he asked all of the questions in turn, it would take up some considerable time, but time was surely something that a woman who apparently didn't work and a university student on his spring break had in abundance. However, he found that she wouldn't give straight answers to questions that shouldn't have been all that hard for someone living in the house, and used lots of vague phrases like *probably* and *I think* and *I'm not sure*. W thought that maybe she wasn't too bright.

'So you and your family are the current residents, I take it? Last time I came I met a little girl by the front door – your little sister maybe?'

She looked up, and without answering placed the empty teacups and plates on the tray. 'Would you like to see around the house?'

That's what he'd come for, he replied. He stood up, scattering pie crumbs on the floor.

Other than the drawing room, there were three further rooms in the Western-style wing of the house, one on the ground floor and two upstairs. A shoddily built shower room somewhat out of keeping with the rest of the house had been added under the stairs, and this made the other ground-floor room seem a little poky compared with the others. Upstairs there was a large master bedroom and another smaller room with a bed in it, possibly for guests.

However, it was not the Western-style wing that made the residence appear somewhat eccentric, but the single-storey Japanese-style house with a veranda that was reached through a dimly lit connecting corridor. What was really strange here was that all the rooms were excessively white; even the ornamental wooden pillar by the traditional alcove had been painted pure white, as had the decorative transom over the sliding doors partitioning the room with an alcove from the one next to it, which had been removed to create one large room. A kitchen cupboard had been inserted into the alcove, and the room furnished with a Western-style dining table and chairs. A carpet had been laid over the tatami in the furthest room, and a big bed placed on it.

'Such bad taste,' the woman said, wrinkling her nose, as W stared in astonishment at the white pillar.

W said nothing, and headed further into the house. All the rooms requiring plumbing had been constructed on the north side, and were separated from the tatami rooms by a corridor. The woman opened an old frosted glass door, and signalled with her thumb for him to enter. Stepping inside, W couldn't help crying out in surprise. There before him was a bath with cabriole legs enshrined in a bathroom tiled entirely in bright yellow. The woman gave a snort of laughter.

'Wow!' W stuttered hesitantly. 'Pretty unique, huh?'

Her eyebrows twitched and she twisted the corners of her lips in a grimace.

Next to the bathroom was the lavatory, which had a Western-style toilet with a wooden lid. In a recess in the corridor there was a black tabletop telephone.

Stranger still, the construction style of the western-most part of the north side looked as though it belonged to a different house entirely, with two small rooms measuring four and a half tatami and three tatami respectively, an extremely modest kitchen, and a lavatory jutting out into the back garden. A small bucket had been hung up to serve as a washbasin, just like those used in the countryside before flushing toilets were introduced.

'This part looks like a completely different house!'

'I heard that they converted what used to be the maids' quarters.'

'The maids' quarters! I guess they would have needed maids in a house this size.'

W looked at the two tiny rooms.

They were both empty of furniture.

It was quite a large residence for the centre of Tokyo, so he had supposed that it was the property of someone with considerable wealth, but even so the maids' quarters were big enough to accommodate a family. 'Shall we go back? I'll pour some more tea,' the woman said.

He didn't want any more of that sickly sweet pie, but he happily complied when she grabbed his wrist and pulled him along after her. He couldn't care less what happened to that blank questionnaire.

THE WOMAN'S NAME was Noriko, she told him. The house apparently was not hers.

The owner and his family were presently living abroad somewhere, and had left her to look after the house alone. That would explain why her answers had been so vague, since she didn't know anything about it, W thought. He didn't think it would be a big problem if he failed to complete the questionnaire for just one house out of several dozen. After all, there were plenty of properties where it was even more difficult to get any data. All he wanted now was to see her again, so he filled in the questionnaire with appropriate answers and submitted it to his workplace, then promptly forgot about anything and everything to do with the survey.

The good thing about the owner being away was that Noriko had the upstairs bedroom to herself. After taking a shower in the small room under the stairs, he wrapped a large towel around himself and, barefooted, followed her up the stairs and into the bedroom, where the bed loomed enormous, so well made it could have been a hotel.

'The first thing I learned when I came here was how to make a bed. You cover a feather mattress with a large sheet and tuck it in, then place another large sheet on top. Blankets are scratchy next to the skin, you see. So you get between the sheets, like this.'

W had never heard of a feather mattress before. Of

course he understood what she meant, though. Noriko
sometimes used strange words – but of course he didn't
care about that, either. Her skin was velvety between the
cool sheets, and his consciousness was entirely focused on
her legs and belly and nipples and neck, and on the soft,
moist opening between her legs.

Afterwards, he was overcome by an agreeable drowsi-
ness. She got up, and he savoured the feeling of being
alone in that bed. It was the largest he'd ever slept in in
his life. When he woke up, the house was enveloped in an
aroma of spices and meat broth.

For a nineteen-year-old student from the provinces,
who existed day-to-day on a small allowance and a
part-time job, Western food meant curry rice or cheap
hamburgers, so this smelled like heaven to him. Noriko
brought him the meal on a silver platter, just like they did
in American movies for a child's birthday, and placed it
atop his quilt-covered thighs as he wriggled into a semi-
upright position on the bed.

She had made something she called chicken casserole.
He asked her what 'casserole' meant, but she replied
sulkily 'I don't know,' and pouted. 'It's the easiest recipe.
You just fry some vegetables and chicken, then tip in a can
of Campbell's cream soup. You can put some cheese on
top if you like, but I just scattered some breadcrumbs on it,
bunged it in the oven for fifteen minutes, and hey presto.'

She'd made the breadcrumbs herself from stale bread
instead of buying them. To his surprise, she'd also made
the bread herself. She served the casserole with white rice
and a side salad of julienned carrots mixed with grapefruit.

When he praised her cooking she replied, 'Well, I have studied up on it, you know.'

A thick book titled *The American Way of Housekeeping* lay beside the bed. On the cover was a picture of smoked salmon covered in green peas, or something of the sort.

In addition to his job with the estate agents, W was also working weeknights as a night watchman at a warehouse in Koto Ward on the other side of the city, which meant that he had to set off from Harajuku at 8p.m. He didn't feel the least inclination to leave her side and pass along glittery Omotesando and catch a train bound for the dreary, empty warehouse. Despite his reluctance, though, she would see him off to the front door and brusquely close the door behind him.

He never met Noriko outside the house. He always visited her there, said goodbye, and that was the end of it. Whenever he tried suggesting going out somewhere together, she would respond 'No, I don't want to,' her white brow furrowing. 'I don't feel like going anywhere. I don't want to leave this house.'

'Not even Yokohama or Kamakura? I can probably borrow a car from a friend. Well, it's his dad's car. I got my licence when I went back home last summer.'

'What? No way. I'm too scared to go with someone not used to driving.'

'Well, we can go by train then. How about taking a ride on the Enoden coastal railway?'

'I said I don't want to.'

'Why?'

'Like I said, I don't want to leave this house.'

Eventually he gave up asking her out. There wasn't really any need to go anywhere, after all. Being in the house they had a shower and a bed, and he got to eat her delicious home-cooked food. She liked to drink Coca-Cola in bed, and he would grab the bottle from her hand, drink it down in one, then roll on top of her again.

ONE AFTERNOON, W happened to be passing not far from the house, so he dropped by and rang the doorbell, but she didn't answer. *She must be out*, he thought, and sat down on the stone step by the front door and read a book while he waited, but she still hadn't come home by the time it was getting dark.

He stood up, thinking he might as well go home and call her later from work at the warehouse. As he went out into the lane beyond the concrete wall, he saw a woman standing there.

'Did you see that girl?' she asked.

He wasn't sure if she was talking to him and tried to carry on past her, but she caught hold of his arm. She was emaciated and looked worn out. How old could she be, he wondered ... maybe about sixty?

'You've seen that girl, haven't you?' she repeated.

'If you mean the person who lives here, she seems to be out at the moment,' he said. He felt a bit spooked by this old woman and tried to shake his arm free.

She closed her eyes and shook her head. 'That's not what I mean. The girl. You've seen her, haven't you?'

The memory of the little girl he'd met replayed in the back of his mind. The pretty girl in her best clothes whom he'd met the first time he'd come to this house.

'You mean the little girl with the pageboy haircut?'

'She's a ghost, you know,' the woman said.

The sun had gone down and the street was shrouded in darkness. This old woman, who obviously had grey hair coloured with cheap dye, was really creepy. She was more like a ghost, he thought, and wrenched his arm free of her grasp.

'She's a ghost, you know,' the woman muttered again, as if to convince herself.

'Give me a break. I didn't come here to listen to that sort of thing.'

'But you should listen.'

'Why?'

'Because once you've seen her, you'll keep seeing her over and over again.'

W broke free from her and went out into Omotesando. It was the same bright and cheerful thoroughfare as always.

He ran into that thin woman with the orangey hair again a few days later.

His life had been abruptly and painfully disrupted. He kept phoning Noriko, but she didn't answer. For want of anything better to do, he went over to the house, but she wasn't at home. Thinking that she was just pretending to be out, he went around the garden to the veranda and banged on the storm shutters, and called out loudly to her, to no avail. At the weekend he had even sat on the stone step by the front door waiting for her through the night until it was nearly light. There were no mobile phones or computers in those days, so he couldn't even email her.

W went to the Harajuku house daily, as if possessed. The word *stalker* didn't exist back then, and he was incapable of seeing objectively that what he was doing was odd. At first he'd thought she must have gone away somewhere, but after a while he began to worry that something must have happened to her. And at some point he began to think that maybe he'd been dumped. With his thoughts swinging wildly back and forth like a pendulum, he kept going back to the house again and again.

And so he ran into the thin woman once again.

'Where did she go?' W lost no time in asking her.

The woman didn't hesitate, either. 'Over there, I'd have thought,' she told him.

'Over there?'

'The other world.'

'You mean she's dead?'

'That's what I told you, isn't it? That girl's a ghost, that's what I said.'

'But I'm not asking about that little girl!'

'But you should. You should listen, like I said.'

W gave a deep sigh, and listened to what she had to say.

'That girl was a distant relative of the wealthy man who lived in this house. Her father died fighting in the war, and she had evacuated with her mother up north to

Tohoku where they both caught dysentery. But her soul could not rest, and she came back to this house where she'd often come to play as a child. Her own house had been one of many demolished to create a firebreak. It was rented and nothing special, so this house was the only place in Tokyo that she felt an attachment to. Whenever she came here she was always given delicious treats to eat. That's why she always wore her best clothes when she visited.'

'When was that?'

'Before the war.'

'That's over forty years ago!'

'Well, that's when it was.'

'What do mean by a firebreak?'

'During the bombing raids on Tokyo, they would demolish all the houses in certain areas in advance to stop fires from spreading. Lots of houses were demolished for that reason.'

'Did you know her?'

The woman nodded.

'And you've seen her since she became a ghost?'

'Many times.'

W pictured the girl in his mind. She hadn't looked at all like a ghost; she had been very real.

'Why are you telling me all this?' he asked, turning to look at her, but he wasn't sure if she was listening.

'She has a strong attachment to this place, so she comes back,' she repeated.

W was getting fed up with the old woman's mutterings, so he left her and took himself off to work.

When he arrived at the warehouse, the telephone rang. He picked up the receiver to hear Noriko's breezy voice on the line. He felt relief, and the next moment anger welled up in him.

'Idiot! Where have you been?' he yelled.

Taken aback, she hung up on him. Immediately he regretted having said that, and fretted away the night waiting impatiently for dawn to come. As soon as he finished work, he jumped straight on a metro train, and ran along Omotesando, almost deserted at that hour, all the way to the house.

Woken from her sleep, Noriko smiled and said, 'So who's the idiot?' and all the tension he'd been feeling for so long drained away. Unable to restrain himself, he took her straight back to bed and held her close.

Now there was an element of mystery about her, W couldn't just let things be, and he started going to see her at any possible opportunity, using the time he would normally spend with friends or on his own hobbies.

When he asked her where she had been, she said she had been visiting her parents in the countryside. When he pressed her for more details, such as where they lived, and was one of her parents ill, and why didn't she at least call him, she responded simply with a smile as though making fun of him. At this point, W had already lost. She no longer attached much importance to him.

'There's no need to visit me every day, you know,' she told him, her voice gentle but firm. 'I'm tired. It's too much. And you already know, don't you? The owner will be coming back soon, so we won't be able to meet like this any more.'

This was a big setback, but more importantly W had begun to suspect her.

She must be going to meet someone else! Or perhaps another man was coming here? And she never knew when he would be coming, which was why she was so adamant about not leaving the house. She had probably spent these past five days with him. And apart from anything, what was her relationship with her employer?

'What's the owner like?' W asked casually, leaning back in the bed pretending to be at ease.

She frowned. 'Why are you bringing that up again?'

Again? W was utterly unable to relax now. Had he really asked that question so many times?

'Does he have a family?'

'A wife and one daughter. They're away with him.'

'How did you get this job?'

'Oh really, you do go on. Why are you asking that? They advertised for someone.'

He could hardly continue on this subject now she'd said that. His jealousy would be too obvious, and for all he knew he might have good reason to be jealous – there might be another man, and he might even be her employer.

Whenever she was in a good mood, she would bake a pie. That awful sweet taste had grown on him and now he was addicted to it. After spending a lazy after-noon eating pie and dozing in bed, it was really hard to drag himself away and go back to that dreary warehouse district. If he called from work and she didn't answer, he felt like he was going crazy.

W tortured himself with foolish fancies. Was her employer even married? Or maybe he was in only Tokyo during the week for work and went back to his family at weekends. On weekdays after work he would go back to the house, and they would together have dinner at the large table that was so out of place in the tatami room, have a bath in the bathroom that was in such bad taste, and spend the night in that bed placed on top of the carpet that had been laid so boorishly in the white-painted Japanese room.

Come to think of it, he had no idea what was going on in that house at night. He realised this with a start, and spent the rest of the night anguishing about it alone in the deserted warehouse in Koto Ward.

It was torture spending all night from nine at night until seven the next morning in the warehouse. He could hardly sleep any more.

He called her daily, and sometimes she was in, sometimes not. When she wasn't, he would be assailed by anxiety and call over and over again. Being unable to go over to see her exacerbated his anguish. Eventually the flabbergasted accounts manager banned him from using the telephone late at night. Until then, though, he'd been able to use the warehouse phone as much as he liked, and would already be dialling the number before he knew what he was doing. At first he'd hesitated to call her at night, but when she didn't answer he stopped caring if he was bothering her. However, when she sometimes answered, sounding sleepy, he would apologise abjectly, but just the thought of hearing her voice would eventually have him reaching for the phone again.

Late one night, after a long period of not connecting, he finally got through. He heard something that could have been a little scream, or a sigh.

'Hey, what's up? Has something happened?' He adjusted his grip on the grey receiver.

There was an odd crackling, like the static on a radio when it can't pick up a signal. He could also hear what sounded like a conversation, although he couldn't make out what was being said.

'Hey, answer me will you? What's going on?'

Answer me! His own voice echoed strangely in his ear. He wasn't even sure who he was expecting to answer him.

After a while he suddenly understood. The conversation on the other end of the line was in a foreign language: the voices of a man and a woman, loud as if having a fight, and then someone's – yes, the woman's – was mixed with the sound of sobbing or shouting in ecstasy. It was almost certainly a crossed line, but W couldn't believe it was simply a technical fault. He hurriedly checked that nothing was out of the ordinary in the warehouse, and left. The first workers would arrive in about two hours, and there was no reason to think anything serious would happen in that time, he decided.

He caught the first train to Harajuku. Few people were up and about at that early hour, and both the main avenue and the backstreets were shrouded in silence, as though still asleep. Once at the door, he lost his nerve and couldn't bring himself to ring the bell. He contemplated whether he should simply sit there and wait for her to come or give up and go home, but then on a whim he went round to the Japanese wing.

The shutters were open and a light was on inside. He stepped uneasily up onto the veranda. Thanks to the frame being well waxed, the glass door slid smoothly open without a sound.

Without further ado W sneaked inside, his nerves uncontrollably on edge. The corridor was cool, and the bizarrely decorated white room was empty. But the light was coming from further inside the house, on the north side. 'Hey, are you there?' W called out as he approached the tatami room there.

'I'm here,' he heard a voice say.

Unsure whether she sounded surprised or angry, he slid the door open, then stared at her aghast.

Before him stood the skinny old woman.

'WHAT ARE YOU DOING HERE?' W asked after a few moments, recovering his power of speech.

'That's what I should be asking you,' the woman said. 'This is my place, after all.'

'Wasn't the owner a man? A man with a family.'

'Depends when you're talking about.'

'When? What do you mean, when?'

'This place was requisitioned by the occupation forces over thirty years ago.'

'Occupation forces?'

'There's a mark left from the old nameplate by the front door. Didn't you see it?'

Now that she mentioned it, he had the feeling that maybe he had seen it, but he didn't quite understand what she was getting at. And coming across her here at this strange hour felt so unreal that everything appeared out of the ordinary to him.

The woman indicated to him that he should sit down at the low table, so he did and awkwardly sipped the tea she poured for him.

'I told you, didn't I? She's a ghost.'

'I haven't met that girl since that first time, you know.'

'I'm not talking about that little girl.'

'But you were the one who brought up the ghost.'

'Yes. What I'm saying is that the little girl and the woman you've been seeing are one and the same.'

'What do you mean?'

'What I said. The girl is a distant relative of the owner of this house, and fell ill after she was evacuated to the countryside. She hovered between life and death, but her attachment to life was strong. After the war, she came back here in that form.'

'In that form?'

'In her adult form, of course.'

'But that's weird, isn't it? Ghosts come back in the same form they had when still alive. I've never heard of a ghost actually growing older.'

'I'm not all that knowledgeable about ghosts myself. But I never said a word about her having died as a child.'

'But you said she fell ill after being evacuated!'

'That's right, with dysentery. Her mother died, but she survived. When the war ended, she ran away from the area she'd been evacuated to and came back to Tokyo. And having learned that this house still stood, she came back here. Not only that, but she used her connections to get a position as housemaid to the American lieutenant living here.'

'But that doesn't fit with her age.'

'Doesn't fit with whose age? She evacuated when she was fourteen, and three years later she would have been seventeen.

'So she's younger than me?'

'Don't be silly, she's much older than you!'

W burst out laughing. He didn't believe a word of what this woman was saying, and neither did he want to. Just the fact he was talking with her as though he did believe her was weird enough – not to mention the way they were talking about such things here in this house. Maybe he'd gone a bit strange in the head, he thought.

She had been seventeen when she'd returned to this house in the summer of 1947.

The owner had converted the maids' quarters for himself and his family and lived there a while, but he couldn't bear to see the foreigners with their different customs installed in the main house and acting as though they owned the place, so they'd moved to a small house he'd found on the Shonan coast, near Kamakura. Noriko hadn't visited them there, but had come straight here to this house. Her relatives up north hadn't been at all kind to her, and having escaped them she was not of a mind to repeat the experience with other relatives, the elderly woman said sympathetically. In those days, any girl who lost her guardian at the age of fifteen or sixteen had to make her own way in life.

Thanks to the good offices of the man in charge of requisitioned houses, she discovered they were looking for a housemaid, managed to get an interview, and moved in. After a while, the lieutenant's wife grew to dislike life in the Far East and went back to her own country with her child, and before she knew it Noriko found herself in the role of the lieutenant's local wife. Or maybe she had been the cause of the lieutenant and his wife falling out. She changed her name to Nora, and began curling her hair.

Nora lived in this house for five years, up to 1952, and during that time she terminated three pregnancies. The lieutenant did not want any children with her and said he would leave her if she insisted on giving birth, so she visited a backstreet doctor who would undertake illegal abortions. The first two times the doctor did the deed without a word, but the third time even he hinted that her life would be in danger. Nevertheless, she insisted she couldn't give birth and went ahead with the operation, but she fell sick and was confined to bed.

When the lieutenant abandoned his bedridden local wife and left for a new posting, she inevitably had to leave the house too. Her distant relative was eventually able to return to the Harajuku house, his honour restored after his exile in Shonan. He made a fortune selling synthetic fibre, but what with the curse of his untimely death and the profligacy of his children, the house and land was taken as security. Eventually it was slated for demolition and a rope prohibiting entry was placed around the property.

'I think the woman you've been seeing is Nora, you know.'

W didn't know what to think.

Of course, he wasn't of a mind to believe what this woman was telling him. Anyway, with her weird hair colour and being so painfully thin, she herself looked more like a ghost.

'You're the one who's giving me the creeps,' he snapped at her angrily. 'What is all that about Nora? Give me a break. And anyway, just who are you? A grandchild of the original owner, are you? Frittered away your inheritance, or something?'

'It's up to you whether you believe me or not,' she muttered offhandedly, and sipped her tea.

What with not having slept all night and the crazy story he'd just had to listen to, W's head felt muddled. He went home to his apartment. He tried phoning again, but Noriko didn't answer, and neither did that weird woman.

AS IT HAPPENED, he wasn't able to go back to the house for the next two weeks. His father suddenly collapsed from a stroke and he was summoned back home immediately, and was busy for some time arranging the wake and funeral. Even so, he still managed to find some time every day to call her, but he never got through.

The last time W visited the house was at the beginning of April when he went to the university to submit a leave of absence. Cherry blossoms were blooming all over the city and were just beginning to scatter. W recalled the tight buds on the cherry tree in the garden.

Turning left off Omotesando into the backstreets, he had to squeeze past construction vehicles blocking the way. And as he got closer to the house, he was left dumbfounded. The grubby grey concrete wall was no longer there, and not only had that tropical-looking windmill palm and the nandina and camellia, the stone lanterns in the garden and the pond with carp swimming in it all gone, but so had the buildings – the Western-style wing, Japanese wing and the corridor connecting them. Everything was gone. All he could see before him now was an empty lot.

'What are you doing? Where's the person who was living here?' he pressed a young man in work clothes, almost grabbing hold of him. But the guy just shoved out his chest belligerently and glared at him. Another man further away, in cleaner work clothes, came running over and introduced himself as the person in charge. What was the problem?

'What happened to the house that was here? Where's the person who was living in it?'

'I was told that nobody was living here. The estate agents hired us to clear the lot, so if there's a problem please bring it up with them,' the man said civilly, although he was clearly annoyed.

When W called the estate agent, the man who answered the phone was surprisingly forthcoming with the details. The property had been state-owned for some time now, and the accommodation for public servants built in the 1960s had been empty for some two years. The land had now been sold to a private developer, who was to build a new condo on it. He asked whether W was sure he wasn't talking about a different property, and double-checked the address several times. There was nothing matching the description of the Kimoto house at that address; there must be some misunderstanding, he said apologetically. W could no longer remember what had been recorded for that address on the map he'd been given when he'd first started that part-time job.

The cherry blossoms in Yoyogi Park were beginning to scatter, bringing back for him the time about a month and a half ago when those trees had still been bare. Ultimately, though, it felt as though he'd been abruptly cut off from everything he'd experienced in that time and place, and it had all vanished.

He handed in his leave of absence at the university and went back home to Oita. Then it was decided he would take over his father's small factory, so he withdrew from university altogether and hardly ever went back to Tokyo after that. As time went by it all began to feel like a dream; the house and Noriko, the little girl, the old woman, the palm tree in the garden, all of it.

Thirty years had gone by, and it was already the time of the future that Marty McFly visited together with Doc in the DeLorean, when W found a short entry in a book titled *Study of Homes in Central Tokyo Requisitioned by the US Military During the Occupation* that he came across in the library.

> Kimoto Residence (Harajuku): Residence of the owner of Kimoto Fabrics, Ltd, completed 1928. Requisitioned by the US military from February 1946 to June 1952. Relatively small for a requisitioned property, with a building of 237m^2 situated on a 653m^2 lot. An eclectic residence comprising a Western-style wing and Japanese-style wing connected by a corridor. No longer in existence. No photographs.

His work file slipped from under his arm and fell to the floor. The librarian looked up at the sound. He bent down to pick up the file but sank to the floor and was unable to get up again, and the small woman came running over to see what was wrong, a concerned look on her face.

—

'SO THE WOMAN CALLED NORIKO and the little girl were ghosts?' one of the assembled party ventured.

'What about that old woman?'

'She was also probably one of the ghosts living in that old house. Like, the daughter of the original owner, or something. That's it, isn't it, W?'

'You may be right, but now, thirty years later, I'm wondering if that old woman was actually Noriko too,'

W said. 'I probably met Noriko at ten years old, Noriko in her twenties and Noriko in her late fifties. That elderly woman was Noriko herself in 1985. She was the only one that I actually met, and somehow I feel maybe I got into her head.'

Even accepting that the Kimoto residence was built in 1928, if it was demolished and accommodation for government workers was built in the '60s, then in 1985 it can't still have been there in Harajuku, W said. If the building had still existed at that time, then I would simply have met the ghosts in it. But since that's not the case, I have no idea where it was that I was visiting so often. Either I was in somebody's dream, or I went to a parallel world with a portal in daily life.

'The only coherent explanation I can think of is that Noriko, now in her fifties, heard that the bulldozers were returning to the site, and so she came to see it. I believe a resonance occurred with her reminiscences, and it so happened I was able to experience with her the scene of her memories.'

I have no idea if such a thing is possible, however. Or whether it's possible for people to see ghosts. Which is the more believable? The glass of whisky in his hand shook as his gaze took on a faraway quality, as though he were lost in his memories. And all of us there found ourselves drawn in with him.

The Last Obon

'SIS SAYS SHE CAN'T COME,' reported Satsuki. 'She has to go to Samezu with Tomoharu.'

'What's in Samezu again?' asked Kayo from the other end of the line, her voice fading in and out. Satsuki imagined her younger sister standing over the stove, the receiver wedged precariously between her cheek and left shoulder as she stirred a pot on the stove.

'Really, Kayo. Samezu is Tomoharu's family home. This year is his father's first Obon,' said Satsuki.

'Oh, yeah. He died in June, right? I couldn't make it to the funeral but I sent my condolences. Did you go?'

'Of course I did,' Satsuki replied. 'You wouldn't *believe* the crowd – I was astounded.'

'In any case, you'd think Sis could still come up to Gunma for a day at least,' said Kayo. 'It's not all *that* far.'

'I suppose it wouldn't be the done thing,' said Satsuki. 'That's what happens when you marry up like that. Apparently, Tomoharu's relatives are going to discuss how to divvy up his father's estate. Sis is in a real to-do over it – you know how she gets about that sort of thing.'

'Sis' was Fumie, the eldest of the three sisters, seven years older than Satsuki and ten more than Kayo. Due to this age gap there had always been an emotional distance between Fumie on one side and Satsuki and Kayo on the other. Besides, there was a sternness to Fumie the other two lacked; over the years the gulf between her and her two younger sisters had only widened.

Kayo let out a deep sigh. She could imagine exactly the state her eldest sister was in.

'Well, then,' she said at last, 'I guess it's just you two and my lot. Ayumi has to write a report for school about how she spent the summer holidays; she wants to write about Obon. Atsushi's missing the first night but he's promised to join me and the kids on the fourteenth. Anyway, I need him to bring the car so he can drive us all back to Tokyo. You know how I detest driving.'

'How are you and the kids getting there?' asked Satsuki.

'We'll take the train from Ueno.'

'I'm going by car. Why don't you come with me?'

'Are you kidding?' said Kayo. 'The roads will be jammed.'

'You think so?'

'Trust me – the train's *way* easier! I'll buy you a ticket and we can all go together.'

'Thanks,' said Satsuki, 'but Masaru has offered to drive me up on the night of the twelfth so we miss the worst of the traffic.'

'You mean he's got all three days off?'

'Apparently his replacement will have started work by then so he won't really have anything to do,' said Satsuki. 'Why, are you calling him a slacker?'

'No, not at all – good for him!' said Kayo. 'And lucky you!'

Laughing like schoolgirls, the two sisters said their goodbyes and rang off.

Satsuki ate dinner alone. When she was done, she ran her eye over the list of things she needed: candles, incense, altar lanterns (was there perhaps still a pair at her mother's old house?), rice dumplings, a bouquet of flowers, a rice-straw mat, and several sprigs of hozuki – Chinese lantern plant – whose bright orange fruit pods, like a string of miniature paper lanterns, made them a favourite Obon decoration.

After their mother's death, Satsuki had inherited the Buddhist altar cabinet containing their ancestors' mortuary tablets. She would take it back to Gunma with her in the car for Obon, but afterwards they would have to decide what to do with it when Satsuki and her husband moved to South Africa in the autumn. They could hardly take it with them and Kayo would probably say her flat was too small.

That left Fumie. But Satsuki doubted she would agree to take it off her hands given the fuss her big sister made about everything. There was nothing Fumie hated more than someone else being in charge, as her two younger sisters knew only too well. It was Kayo who had given Satsuki the idea of letting Fumie suggest it herself. 'The only way Sis will agree to it is if she thinks it was her idea in the first place,' Kayo said. Satsuki was the one who had proposed celebrating Obon at the Gunma house for old times' sake. For that reason alone, right from the start, she had half expected Fumie to say she wouldn't come.

Their mother had been born and raised in a small town in Gunma Prefecture, a couple of hours north-west of Tokyo by car. Her elder brother had taken over the family home and when he died his wife had lived alone there for many years. Then, when she eventually passed away, their mother had inherited the old wooden Japanese-style house where she had grown up, though it was by then quite dilapidated and she rarely went there. But from time to time she seemed to suddenly remember its existence and decide that it needed a good cleaning.

After their father died, their mother announced her intention to return to her birthplace to live out her final years. Fumie had been adamantly opposed to her living in the countryside all on her own, of course, but their mother had gone ahead and done it anyway. But she never again celebrated Obon in the Gunma house as they had in the old days. Come mid-August, she would go and lay flowers on the family grave at the local temple, but after decades of marriage and motherhood, it seemed the traditional observances had become too much trouble. On top of that, she had to come to Tokyo during Obon to visit her husband's grave.

Then three years ago their mother had passed away suddenly, leaving her childhood home to her three grown-up daughters. The ramshackle old house buried deep in the countryside had not even merited any inheritance taxes. Fumie had wanted to sell up right away, divide the meagre proceeds and be done with it. But her two more sentimental siblings had insisted on holding onto the house, at least for a while, in memory of their mother.

The job of watching over the old house had fallen to Satsuki and her husband, Masaru. Fumie lived too far away and Kayo was busy raising two small children. But having learned that Masaru's company was transferring him in the autumn to its office in South Africa, Satsuki had to face the fact that the time had finally come to let the house go. So she and her husband went to talk to the local estate agent, and before they knew it a buyer was found. The sale was to be finalised at the end of August and the house demolished in September to make way for a convenience store.

The idea of holding a family gathering over the summer holidays to bid farewell to the old house had come up in the middle of July. The timing seemed too good to let pass. Satsuki suggested to Kayo they celebrate a traditional Obon, the annual commemoration of the ancestors, at the Gunma house, as they did when they were children. Her younger sister agreed immediately. There was just one problem: what *was* a traditional Obon exactly? They couldn't quite remember, nor could they think of anyone, such as an elderly neighbour, to ask.

Growing up, the three sisters had been taken to Gunma every August for Obon until about the time Kayo was ready to start school. By then Satsuki was halfway through the primary grades. Her memories, though clear in some respects, were not a hundred per cent reliable. Fumie, being the oldest by seven years, undoubtedly had the best recollection of those days, but without her on hand to help out, Satsuki and Kayo were afraid that it might not be a 'proper' Obon.

Their father had been born in Shimane, in south-western Japan, but he had rarely gone back to visit his parents, even at holidays. For the three sisters, then, summer vacation – when families typically visited relatives in the countryside – meant their mother's old house in Gunma. In those days their maternal grandmother was still alive and lived in the house with their mother's elder brother and his wife, who had no children. In those days, Obon had always been a true Obon.

Their mother had been one of three children. In addition to their uncle in Gunma, she had had a younger brother who visited the old house one summer with his young bride and baby girl while the sisters were staying there. But he and his small family had emigrated to Brazil some time back, and the sisters had no idea what had become of this other uncle and his daughter, possibly their one and only cousin.

Upon entering high school, Fumie announced that she was no longer willing to join her parents and siblings on any outings. At that point their family trips had ceased. For a while, during Obon, their mother would take her two younger daughters to Gunma for the day to visit the family grave. But after their uncle passed away it didn't seem worth the trouble, and their mother began leaving the two of them behind and going on her own. Then their uncle's widow had died as well, followed not too many years after by their mother. And thus they had got to where they were now.

For Satsuki, the impression of Obon that existed in her childhood memories was of a lively and almost festive occasion. Her grandmother's brothers and sisters would come, as would their children and their children's children. She remembered playing with little boys and girls her own age who might have been distant cousins of one kind or another. She remembered neighbours dropping by unannounced, saying they had come 'to offer a stick of incense for the ancestors' at the family altar.

The old house had a veranda that overlooked a small garden. A memory flitted into Satsuki's mind, like a scene from some movie she might have seen long ago, of an old man sitting on the edge of the veranda, while her aunt, wearing a long-sleeved white smock, said a few words to him as she offered him a glass of cold barley tea. Satsuki also saw an image of her wizened, silver-haired grandmother in a summery dress of bluish grey crêpe, kneeling on the tatami slowly fanning herself, her legs tucked decorously under her, her bottom resting on the upturned soles of her feet and her back doubled over with age.

But for Satsuki the round paper fans her grandmother kept in the house to relieve the August heat had had a different purpose: to drive away the smell of incense. Even now nothing conjured up memories of the Gunma house, which she had always visited only in summertime during Obon, so readily as the smell of altar incense. She had abhorred it as a child and even now did not much care for the cloying scent.

ON THE MORNING OF THE TWELFTH, Masaru, Satsuki's husband, announced that he probably wouldn't be driving up that night after all. 'I thought we could go tomorrow,' he suggested instead.

'But I wanted to go tonight so I can start getting things ready in the morning,' replied Satsuki. 'Kayo and the kids will be arriving after lunch and I want to be sure to be there first.'

But Masaru insisted he needed to be at work that day.

'Fine, I'll go alone, then,' said Satsuki, a bit huffily, as she left the house.

Satsuki did not want to leave for Gunma without first paying a visit to her parents' graves. Long ago, her father had purchased a burial plot at a temple in Chofu, on the western outskirts of Tokyo. At the time her parents had been living at Tobitakyu, one stop beyond Chofu on the Keio commuter rail line from Shinjuku. It must have seemed a good idea back then, but today none of the three sisters lived anywhere near the Keio line, let alone as far afield as Chofu.

Normally Satsuki didn't bother with the Obon observances and only visited her parents' graves on their death anniversaries or when it suited her. But as she was going to be away in the countryside for Obon this year, it worried her to think of her parents' spirits returning from the other world and finding her not at home. So she had decided to visit their graves before leaving, explain the situation, and invite them, if it wasn't too much trouble, to come to Gunma to see everyone.

It had been her mother's dying wish that half of her ashes be buried in Chofu with her husband, and half in Gunma with her ancestors. Such, it seemed, was her fondness for her old home and her desire that her daughters look after the family grave.

Satsuki returned from Chofu in the afternoon to pack. In the evening, her husband called to say that he would indeed be working late and to go on ahead without him. Satsuki ate dinner alone.

So much for her husband's promise to drive her up, thought Satsuki; it was too late to take the train, and she had too much stuff to carry anyway. The holiday traffic out of Tokyo would already be well underway, so she waited until eight o'clock to avoid the worst of it before setting off. It was nearly ten by the time she pulled up outside the old house in the countryside.

She walked up the path to the front door in pitch darkness, training her tiny keyring torch at the ground to see where she was going. The door made a jarring sound as she slid it partway open and slipped through. A musty smell hung about the old house and the air felt cooler than outside. Reaching for a round black object mounted on the wall just inside the entryway, Satsuki flipped the metal switch in the centre upwards. Overhead an incandescent bulb with a shade thickly coated in dust blinked uncertainly for a moment before casting its yellowish light over her.

The narrow entryway consisted of a rough concrete slab. A single breeze block, artlessly put there by her mother when she lived there alone, served as a makeshift step up to the raised floor of the traditional old wooden house. The block wobbled as Satsuki put her weight on it.

The doctors had attributed her mother's death to a cerebral haemorrhage. The newspaper delivery boy found her unconscious on the veranda and she died in hospital three days later. The news that she had been taken to hospital had come as a shock to Satsuki, who had been in the habit of calling her mother on weekends when she could, and going to Gunma to visit her every other month or so at most. She had not imagined something like this might happen so soon. Was it her mother's way of reproaching her for being a bad daughter, for neglecting her and allowing her to live all alone? As soon as her mother was out of hospital, Satsuki resolved, she would bring her back to Tokyo to live with her. But then her mother was gone, just like that. She was only sixty-nine.

This was what went through Satsuki's mind as she made her way down the corridor to the kitchen, filled the kettle and placed it on the gas burner. She had made much progress in clearing out the house, slowly at first after her mother's death, then with a greater sense of urgency once her husband's transfer to South Africa was finalised. Now there was hardly anything left and, though by no means a large house, it felt spacious and empty.

Entering the next room, Satsuki took a futon from the closet, unfolded it and laid it out on the tatami. Then she covered it with a sheet from home and spread a cotton blanket on top for good measure: coming from the sweltering heat and humidity of Tokyo, where it was impossible to sleep without airconditioning, Satsuki always found the summer nights in the countryside surprisingly cool.

With nothing else to do before turning in, she took out her mobile phone and was just about to give her husband or her younger sister a call when she heard the front doorbell. Startled, she glanced up instinctively at the old wooden clock on the wall, which evidently hadn't been wound for some time, as the hands were stuck at three-thirty.

According to her wristwatch it was nearly a quarter to eleven. The doorbell rang a second time. Satsuki got up warily and went out of the room and down the corridor to the entryway. Then for some reason she began to feel afraid and stopped, trying to quieten her breathing.

Just then she heard a voice outside mutter, 'That's odd...' and then more loudly, 'Mrs Kaido ... Auntie, are you at home?'

Though Kaido was her mother's maiden name, Satsuki couldn't imagine that she would have begun using it again after moving back to Gunma. Something didn't feel right. She dialled the police emergency number on her mobile, just in case, and held it in one hand ready to press the 'talk' button if necessary.

'Who is it?' she called out through the door.

'Ah, I *thought* you must be home. It's Mr Tsurumi, Auntie – the son, I mean,' said the voice on the other side.

Satsuki didn't know any Mr Tsurumi, or his son for that matter.

'If you're here to see my mother,' she replied, 'she passed away three years ago.' Satsuki watched the man's shadow on the mottled glass pane of the door as he gave a small gasp. 'Now, if you'll excuse me, it's quite late,' she continued quickly, hoping to get rid of him before he could ask any more questions.

But after a moment's hesitation, the man, very politely, said, 'I've come a long way tonight and must be heading home. I think fate brought me here tonight, of all nights, to learn of your poor mother's unfortunate passing ... I know it's late, but may I come in for a moment to light a stick of incense in her memory?'

'I'm sorry,' she said, 'but the house has been sold and we're in no state to receive visitors – I haven't got so much as a cushion for you sit on...' Then, to make sure he got the message, she lied, 'Anyway, my husband's asleep.'

The man apparently got the message.

'Forgive me,' he said. 'I should have known better ... It's just that your dear mother was very kind to me – after I moved away she made me feel that her door was always open to me. I'm truly sorry to have disturbed you. Please remember me to her in your prayers and tell her Yohei Tsurumi sends his regards.'

As the man turned to go, something stirred in the back of Satsuki's mind.

'Wait ... Yohei?' she blurted out. 'The tofu-maker's son – *that* Yohei?'

'That's right.'

'Hold on a sec.'

Hurriedly, Satsuki unlocked the door. It clattered again as she slid it open and the man turned. He had a handsome head of salt-and-pepper hair and appeared to be around fifty. Indeed, at a glance he easily might have passed for no more than ten years older than herself. And yet the Yohei of her childhood memories had been a man already in the prime of life.

'I'm sorry, it's been so long that I—' he began.

'It's been ages, Yohei! Do you remember? You took me down to the river once or twice to swim when I was little. It's funny, but you're much younger than I expected. I remember you as being nearly middle-aged!'

'Yes, of course!' the man exclaimed. 'You were just a wee thing back then.'

'You're thinking of my younger sister, Kayo. I was already in preschool.'

'Like I said, a wee thing!' he repeated in his lilting Gunma accent, running a hand through his salt-and-pepper hair.

Having opened the door, Satsuki now found it impossible not to invite him in to light a stick of incense before going on his way.

'It's very kind of you,' he said. 'I hope I won't wake your husband.'

'That was just a fib,' laughed Satsuki, showing him through to the sitting room.

The family altar cabinet that she had brought up from Tokyo with her sat where she had left it in the middle of the tatami room, wrapped in its covering of purple cloth.

It was only after removing it that Satsuki remembered she had left the altar candlesticks and incense burner in the car. As she couldn't be bothered to go back outside to get them, she asked Yohei if he didn't mind forgoing the candles, and in lieu of the incense burner she fetched a small water glass from the kitchen. Yohei kneeled in front of the cabinet, lit a stick of incense with his cigarette lighter and placed it on the altar in the empty glass. Then he closed his eyes and prayed silently.

'So you used to visit my mother, you said?' she asked when he was done.

'Yeah,' he said. 'But that was after Dad retired and we closed the family tofu shop.'

'Huh? I thought it was still there, on the corner.'

'Someone runs an organic produce store there now. They've got a tank of fresh tofu out front, just for show. They don't actually make it there like we did.'

Still kneeling, Yohei turned to face Satsuki.

'You see, a long time back I moved away to Suki, where my wife's family lives. Once, when I was back visiting my parents' grave, I ran into your mother in town. We got talking and she invited me over for tea. After that I'd drop by to see her whenever I felt nostalgic for the old days and wanted to see my childhood home – that's when I started calling her "Auntie". I feel awful that I didn't know she'd passed away. A poor way to repay her kindness…'

He again ran his fingers through his salt-and-pepper head of hair.

'So you haven't been back for about three years, then?' asked Satsuki to smooth over his awkwardness.

'Eight, as matter of fact...'

Satsuki almost dropped her cup of tea.

'Eight years!' she exclaimed. 'Hold on ... so all this time you've been talking about Aunt Kaido?'

'Exactly, Auntie Kaido...'

'No, what I mean is, the woman you're referring to wasn't my mother – she was an aunt!'

'Oh, your *mother's* aunt, was she?'

'No...'

They eventually got things sorted out. It had been about thirty years since Yohei had married and moved to Suki, and over twenty since his family closed the tofu shop. It was sometime after that that Yohei had begun having tea with Satsuki's aunt. Eight years ago, he had decided to move his parents' ashes from the local temple to one closer to his home in Suki. He had not been back since.

'I sell imported cars for a living, you see. I got an order recently for a luxury model from some crazy rich bloke who lives off the Tohoku Expressway just north of here. He wanted it delivered before Obon and asked me to drive it up to him, wouldn't take no for an answer. Since I was in the area, I couldn't pass up the chance to see my old home again after all these years, particularly at Obon. Then, as I was driving by, I saw a light on and couldn't resist saying hello to Auntie ... But now I know she's long gone, and your dear mother too ... If you don't mind, I'd like to light a stick of incense for her as well.'

The tofu-maker's-son-turned-car-dealer swivelled around to face the altar. Taking another stick of incense, he lit it and plopped it into the glass beside the first one, which had burned halfway down. Then he bowed his head and prayed.

'So, out of curiosity, who did you think I was at first?' asked Satsuki, when he had finished. 'Because my aunt didn't have any children.'

'Erm, well ... I was rather wondering about that,' replied Yohei, rubbing the salt-and-pepper stubble that covered his chin as well. 'But under the circumstances I didn't want to let on that I didn't know who you were. I figured you must be a relative of some sort.'

His words made Satsuki realise how reckless she had been to open the door to him, and she trembled slightly at the thought of what might have happened. *Thank goodness he turned out to be all right*, she thought to herself.

Then the tofu-maker's son said something that truly surprised her.

'To be honest,' he continued, almost as though making a confession, 'I was struck by what an uncanny coincidence it all was: my passing by, seeing a light on, you answering the door. Being Obon and all it must mean *something*, I thought. Then I remembered Auntie Kaido did have a daughter long ago.'

'Really?'

'Yes,' Yohei nodded seriously, 'but she died.'

'My aunt ... a daughter? I had no idea!'

'Like you, she was just a wee thing when I knew her,' explained Yohei. 'About three, I'd say. I was still a kid myself. I remember her trailing after me and the older kids when we went down to the river.' In Yohei's lilting Gunma accent, it sounded like he said, 'we *waint* down to the river'. 'Sometimes I'd give her a piggyback ride if one of the grown-ups told us to take her along.'

'I don't remember her,' said Satsuki.

'She died quite young.'

'I wonder why I've never heard about her.'

'It must've been long before you were born,' said Yohei. 'People probably didn't like to talk about it. It must've been very painful for your aunt. The girl slipped and fell in the river ... not with me and my friends, mind you. Somehow, she'd gone on her own that day. I had nightmares about it for a long time, actually. I mean, she was just a little kid and she drowned right where we always played. It gave me the chills.'

'I imagine you were too scared to go back there after that.'

'Well, boys being boys, we did – eventually. But I've never quite got over it, even to this day, and with tomorrow being Obon, well ... I thought maybe you *were* Auntie Kaido's daughter, like you said when you answered the door.'

'A ghost, you mean?' Satsuki said incredulously.

'I'm sorry, but it *was* an uncanny coincidence...'

It seemed so fantastical, and the man looked so genuinely contrite about his mistake, that Satsuki couldn't help bursting into laughter.

'I'm sorry, I shouldn't laugh,' she said. 'After all, I *did* say you'd taken me to the river as a child, didn't I? I think I'd have been a bit scared if I'd been in your shoes!'

Yohei laughed too. 'I *was* rather scared, to be honest.'

'But didn't it strike you that if Aunt Kaido's daughter died in childhood her ghost should've been the same age as when she died?'

'That did puzzle me,' admitted Yohei. 'I mean, you're very grown-up!'

They both had a good laugh over that. Then, rising to his feet, Yohei said, 'Well, I mustn't keep you up any longer,' and going to the front door he slipped on his shoes. Satsuki turned on her torch to light the way for him; when they reached her car, he took it from her and shone it at the tyres.

'It's time you had those changed,' he said. 'You could have a nasty accident in the rain. Please drive carefully!'

And with those words of advice he gave a slight bow of the head and disappeared into the night.

SATSUKI SPENT ALL THE NEXT MORNING cleaning the house and hanging the futons out to air.

Having decided they would use just the small sitting room where she had placed the Buddhist altar, as well as the somewhat larger room next to it, Satsuki got down on her hands and knees and scoured the tatami mats with a damp rag. Sleeping six people – four adults and two children – in a space just ten tatami mats in size would be a tight squeeze. Moreover, there were just four futons, so Kayo was bringing sleeping bags for Ayumi and Tsutomu. It reminded Satsuki of summer vacations during her student days, when she and her friends would rent a small cabin together at the beach or in the mountains.

A little past noon, Kayo and the children appeared.

Ayumi was in her third year of primary school. Tsutomu was in kindergarten and would be starting first grade the following April. Seeing her niece and nephew, Satsuki marvelled at how time flew. It would be some time before she returned from South Africa. How much would they have grown the next time she saw them? Leaving their aunt to wallow in these sentimental thoughts, the two children ran out into the garden and began playing.

The tomboyish Ayumi soon discovered a pile of moss-covered paving stones in a corner of the garden, and, using it to clamber onto the wall enclosing the north and west sides of the property, she began walking along the top as though on a balance beam. Her younger brother tried to copy her, but found he was too small and his legs too short. He stamped his feet several times on the ground in frustration before bursting into tears. Heaving a sigh, his mother went over and lifted him onto the wall, whereupon he quickly began tootling along like his sister, seemingly unafraid.

Their childless aunt watched anxiously from the house, trying to tell herself that their play was not as dangerous as it looked. After all, hadn't she loved climbing trees and such when *she* was a child? Some deep emotion stirred in her as an image flitted through her mind of her and her two sisters running around the garden with some children whose names she had long since forgotten. Who was the girl in a red pinafore she was chasing? Satsuki sensed that her real childhood had been gradually overwritten with scenes from movies and

TV shows set in an imagined, nostalgic past, and the unexpected shallowness of her memories appalled her.

Then another image came back to her with vivid realness: her aunt in her long-sleeved white smock, wiping her finger around the edge of a mixing bowl full of sweet bean paste and holding it out for Satsuki to lick. Then her gaze shifted from her aunt to the edge of the veranda, where a boy in short trousers with close-cropped hair stood holding a butterfly net and a cage for trapping insects, and suddenly it too no longer felt like a real scene from her past but something out a comic book.

'You know, I had a peculiar visitor last night,' said Satsuki, turning to Kayo, and she proceeded to tell her younger sister about the visit from the tofu-maker's son. When she was done, Kayo frowned and remarked that it had been unwise to let a stranger into the house late at night.

When they were ready to start decorating the Obon altar, Kayo called the children back inside. Ayumi came racing into the house at once, but Tsutomu, still on top of the wall and unable to climb down on his own, burst into tears again and cried until his mother went and helped him down. Then he insisted on being carried all the way into the house.

'You know, I've completely forgotten how one decorates the altar,' Kayo said to her sister when she returned.

'What I remember best is that we always hung hozuki,' replied Satsuki.

In those days, a large Buddhist altar cabinet the size of an old clothes chest, not the little one their mother had left them, had sat in the small sitting room, and at Obon a sprig of hozuki pods was always hung over the altar doors. Someone – one of the older neighbourhood girls, or perhaps a long-forgotten relative – had shown Satsuki how to carefully remove the fruit and blow into the papery orange pod to make a sound like a croaking frog. A patient child, she would sit for ages gently scrunching and massaging the berry until it could be extracted without damaging the delicate pod. But Kayo would always lose patience after a couple of squeezes and try to force the fruit out, inevitably tearing the pod.

'What about the vegetable animals with chopstick legs?' asked eight-year-old Ayumi, frowning.

'The cucumber horse and aubergine ox? We never did that in our family, did we, Kayo?' replied her aunt, looking to Ayumi's mother for confirmation.

'Not as far as I recall. But if you want to make the horse and ox, dear, go right ahead,' said Kayo, slipping her hand into a plastic shopping bag and taking out each of the vegetables in question.

'But, Ayumi,' her aunt objected, 'didn't you want to write your report on the local customs here in Gunma?'

'But it won't feel like Obon without vegetable animals,' the girl retorted sharply, adding for good measure, 'and I want to float paper lanterns on the river too.'

'People around here don't do that either,' said Satsuki.

'But it's one of Japan's *great cultural traditions* – we learned all about it at school,' the girl said peevishly.

'Anyway, if they don't make vegetable animals and float lanterns, what *do* people do here for Obon?'

It was a good question, one to which Satsuki didn't have a ready answer.

Kayo came to her rescue. 'Well, I suppose they make udon noodles,' she suggested, pushing at her spectacles to stop them sliding down her nose, which was damp with perspiration.

'Udon – how so?' asked Satsuki.

'Don't you remember Mum always saying that no family gathering was complete without homemade udon? People in Gunma love their noodles. Here they say, "There's always room for udon" and "Steamed buns for breakfast and udon for lunch, but rice will do for dinner".'

'But if they eat udon all the time, then it's not specific to Obon,' said Satsuki. 'If anything, when I think of Obon I think of bush clover dumplings.'

'You mean peony dumplings,' said Kayo. 'Bush clover dumplings are for spring and autumn equinox.'

'No,' said Satsuki. 'Peony dumplings are eaten at spring equinox. Bush clover's an autumn flower. Obon's in between, so one can eat either, but usually the latter.'

At this point, Ayumi got fed up and announced she was going to make the animals.

Popular belief held that the fleet-footed horse whisked the ancestral spirits home at the beginning of Obon; when it was over, the lumbering ox carried them back to the other world. Who knew why this custom hadn't caught on in Gunma? Instead people visited their family graves on the first night of Obon with a paper lantern to convey the ancestral spirits home. *All things considered,* pondered Satsuki, *doesn't this make more sense than impaling some vegetables with disposable chopsticks?*

Once the children had finished making the animals, the sisters got out a low folding table; on it they spread Satsuki's rice-straw mat. At one end they placed their mother's altar cabinet, at the other the vegetable animals with their chopstick legs. In between they put a platter piled high with oranges, bananas and a melon, then a small wicker tray with the sweetened rice dumplings. On either side of the altar they placed their aunt's Chinese silk lanterns. Finally, Kayo tied freshly cut stalks of bamboo to each corner of the table, strung twine in between, and hung the sprigs of orange hozuki.

At just after five o'clock, Satsuki left Kayo to start on dinner and set off for the family temple with the children, as her handbook on Obon customs told her: *One should welcome the ancestral spirits home early and send them on their way late at night.*

One memory that stuck with Satsuki after all these years was of her family hurrying along a country road, as dusk closed in, trying to reach the local temple before sunset lest 'the ancestors be left to wander aimlessly after dark'. In those days the road leading to the family temple had been a narrow, pot-holed, tyre-scored dirt track that sent up clouds of dust whenever a pickup truck went past loaded with farm tools. It had long since been paved and widened, and now ran straight to the expressway, rows of cookie-cutter houses on either side having replaced vegetable and paddy fields.

Now, as Satsuki walked along, cautioning her five-year-old nephew, a bag of rice dumplings dangling from his hand, not to go dashing on ahead, she gazed towards the range of mountains rising in the west and remembered seeing the same mountains silhouetted a deepening smoky blue as the sun sank slowly behind them. It gave her a sense of having returned to an old, familiar place.

Upon reaching the temple, they went to the family grave and ladled water over the tombstone from a wooden bucket. The children set the dumplings and the flowers down on the grave and Satsuki lit a stick of incense, then used its glowing tip to light the paper lantern she had brought.

'Ready for the big day?'

Satsuki turned at the sound of the voice. Before her stood a black-robed figure holding a bamboo broom in one hand. Three years before she had met the head priest of the family temple for the first and only time, when she brought her mother's ashes to be interred. *We were wondering if you could come to us for Obon this year*, she ventured over the phone during her last visit. *Of course, anytime!* was his exuberant reply, somewhat to her surprise, for surely the date wasn't up to her, was it? *How about the evening of the fourteenth, then?* she suggested. And so the arrangements were made for him to come and recite the sutras at her mother's old house.

'It's tomorrow,' added the priest for good measure.

'Yes,' said Satsuki.

'Few people bother to visit their family graves during Obon any longer,' he suddenly bemoaned, 'and still fewer ask to have the traditional memorial rites performed. I suppose one must change with the times ... But these days I dare not even preach that neglecting these spiritual duties leads to damnation. Instead I just tell people that occasional prayer will ensure their departed loved ones' eternal happiness ... And still they turn away from the true path! As a man of the cloth, it's encouraging to see young people like yourself returning to the countryside and reviving old traditions. It renews even *my* faith!'

The priest laughed.

'I'm glad to hear that, but unfortunately…' faltered Satsuki.

'Yes?'

'Well, this autumn my husband and I are moving to South Africa and we'll no longer be able to visit the grave. I'm afraid this year's Obon will be our last ... I intended to speak to you about performing the memorial rites in perpetuity on our behalf.'

'Oh, I see,' said the priest, his shoulders slumping slightly. Then, gazing thoughtfully at the two children, who were chasing one another round the tombstone, he abruptly changed the subject. 'Now, when you get home, the first thing you must do, before lighting the altar candles from the lantern containing the ancestral spirits, before even entering the house, is wash your feet.'

'Wash our feet?' Satsuki parroted. But no sooner were the words out of her mouth than she faintly recalled returning from the temple as a child and dipping her tiny feet – or more likely pretending to – into a bucket of water before entering her aunt and uncle's house.

'It's these customs that are being lost,' lamented the priest. 'By the way,' he added, almost as an afterthought, 'do you know on what day the Pot of Hell is opened and sinners are released from their eternal suffering?'

Satsuki looked puzzled. 'I assume it's today – isn't that why Obon begins tonight?'

'Not at all,' replied the priest knowingly. 'In fact, the Pot of Hell is opened on the first day of the seventh lunar month, when the demons who stir the pot take their summer rest. In other words, the ancestral spirits have been wandering this world for two weeks already! Tonight is when they are reunited with the living and taken home to reside in the ancestral altar for the duration of Obon.'

It struck Satsuki that monks said some extraordinary things.

With that the head priest bade them goodnight and the three of them set off, Satsuki urging along the children, who were engrossed in conversation. *Did you want to eat a dumpling? Nope, they looked yucky. What do they taste like? I wouldn't know, I've never eaten one. I bet they'd taste good with some sweet bean paste. I hear these ones are just for dead people* … Listening to them, Satsuki pictured herself as a child chattering away with Kayo in similar fashion.

Back at the house, Kayo, always happiest in the kitchen, was making bush clover dumplings. Satsuki's husband, Masaru, was sprawled out on the floor of the living room reading a paperback.

'Oh, you're here,' said Satsuki.

'I said I'd come on the night of the thirteenth,' replied Masaru, sounding a bit put out. Then, as though remembering something, he added, 'Say, is this house famous around here?'

'Not really. It's just old,' said Satsuki, 'Why?'

'Well, I got lost after getting down from the bus and asked a woman for directions,' explained Masaru. '"Oh, the Kaidos' old house," she said at once and happily told me how to get here.'

'What sort of woman?' asked Satsuki.

'Quite a beauty, to be honest – in an understated way.'

'I wonder who was happier,' teased Kayo, appearing from the kitchen with a plate of bush clover dumplings. 'The beautiful woman giving the directions or the person receiving them?'

Masaru, as though trying to hide his embarrassment at this jibe, grabbed a dumpling off the plate and popped it into his mouth, drawing a protest from Kayo. *Hey, we haven't offered any to the Buddha yet! Too late, I've swallowed it. You're impossible! Now get out a plate and put some on the altar … Children, have you washed your hands?* This exchange too had a familiar ring to Satsuki's ears.

'Did you ask this understated beauty her name?' Satsuki asked her husband.

'No, but she seems to have been a friend of your mother's. She said she'd stop by tomorrow to pay her respects.'

'What, stop by this house?'

'Well, isn't that the custom out here in the sticks?'

said Masaru, reaching for another dumpling, which he evidently approved of.

'It's not Tokyo, that's for sure,' observed Kayo sitting down and doling out some dumplings to the two children.

'You can say that again,' said Satsuki. 'I guess we should expect neighbours dropping by all day tomorrow to pay their respects. I wonder if we have enough tea and dumplings to go around?'

'I don't think *that* many will come,' said Masaru, stifling a yawn and returning to his book. Kayo, meanwhile, was scolding Ayumi and Masaru for licking off all the sweet bean paste and leaving the sticky rice balls underneath untouched.

For dinner they had vegetable curry, a far cry from the traditional vegetarian meal usually eaten at Obon but a necessary concession to the children. After they had been put to bed, the topic of conversation eventually turned back to the 'understated beauty', when out of the blue Masaru suddenly turned to his wife and his sister-in-law and asked, 'Your mother's name was Kimiyo, wasn't it?'

'Yes,' replied Satsuki.

'So who's Teruyuki?'

'No idea.'

'The woman said Kimiyo had a brother named Teruyuki.'

'Is he the one who went off to Brazil?' offered Kayo.

'Oh, I remember now,' said Satsuki. 'Mum did have a younger brother named Teruyuki who emigrated to Brazil.'

'The woman said she and Teruyuki had been close,' said Masaru.

'Hold on – how old *was* she?'

'Hard to say ... forties, I suppose, though she could pass for thirty-something. At any rate, she was quite stunning.'

'So you said.'

'Maybe it was the way she was dressed ... Anyway, if you ask me, I got the distinct impression she and this Teruyuki had a thing once.'

'Well, in that case, surely she'd be in her sixties by now.'

'That's what struck me as strange.'

The sisters, each sipping a can of beer, pressed Masaru about what exactly had led him to think the woman and Teruyuki had 'had a thing once'. In the end, he told them the entire story:

Following Satsuki's instructions, he got onto a bus outside the train station and took it to the stop nearest the house. He had been wandering about trying to get his bearings when the woman appeared from around a corner; he stopped her and asked for directions, pointing to his map. After studying it for a moment, her face suddenly lit up and she asked if he was going to the Kaidos' house. As the name meant nothing to Masaru, he explained that his wife's maiden name was Tachiki and her mother had grown up here but married and moved to Tokyo, returning to her childhood home towards the end of her life and living there until she died.

'Do you mean Kimiyo?' the woman had asked, and when Masaru had replied that, yes, his mother-in-law's first name had been Kimiyo, the woman beamed and said that in that case it was indeed the Kaidos' house he wanted, adding, 'That was Teruyuki's house – I spent many happy times there.'

'She told me Teruyuki was the only man she ever really wanted to marry. Imagine, saying that to a complete stranger! She even put her hand on my arm when she said it.'

'She must be a bit mad, don't you think?'

'That's what I've been trying to say. 'If I'd married Teruyuki,' she said, 'he probably wouldn't have gone off to Brazil. But either way I wouldn't have made a good wife – just look how I ended up…' So I asked her if she'd never married.'

'That was very bold of you,' said Kayo, 'for a complete stranger.'

'Was that bad?' asked Masaru. 'Anyway, she replied, "I did marry, but this is how I ended up, so I suppose I wasn't cut out for it." I guess her marriage ended in divorce,' he concluded.

The conversation came to an abrupt end. A quiet breeze drifted into the room, carrying with it the chirping of crickets from the thicket of tall grass at the bottom of the garden.

'It doesn't make sense,' said Satsuki. 'Uncle Teruyuki was quite a bit younger than Mum, but nevertheless he was a good ten years older than Fumie. Assuming he went off to Brazil right after university, even if this ex-girlfriend of his was twenty at the time, she must be over fifty now.'

'I don't know,' said Kayo. 'Plastic surgery's awfully good these days. Actresses never grow old. Nobody looks their real age.'

'Perhaps she was a ghost,' suggested Masaru. The two women eyed him dubiously. 'I mean, it being Obon and all,' he added, grinning.

'Give me a break!' 'Are you trying to scare us?' the two women scoffed.

'But that reminds me...'

Satsuki proceeded to tell Kayo and Masaru about how she had been mistaken for a ghost the previous night by Yohei. They all had a good laugh over that.

THE NEXT MORNING, Satsuki and Kayo went into town for the 'Obon flower market', having read in the paper that a market selling vegetables, plants and flowers for decorating the traditional Obon altar would be held near the station. It turned out to be a small and rather sad affair in a corner of the run-down high street, where a number of folding tables had been set up, with rice-straw mats thrown over them and the vendors' wares haphazardly laid out. The vegetables, displayed in rustic wicker baskets, were small but pleasing to the eye: clearly superior in quality to what Kayo had bought at the local supermarket, but not sufficiently so as to make her want to buy any. She settled instead on an assortment of autumn flowers and grasses, and two large lotus leaves.

'How's business?' she said conversationally to the man helping her, wondering at how few other people there were at the market.

'Worse and worse every year,' he grumbled in the slight lilting accent that indicated he was one of the locals.

Back home, when they had all finished eating lunch, Masaru offered to take the children down to the river. Satsuki began to fret, recalling Yohei's story of the little girl – the niece she had never known – who had drowned there.

'Don't worry, Mother,' said Tsutomu, sounding very grown-up. 'It's not like we're going alone.'

'Remember, you mustn't fish, since it's Obon,' Kayo cautioned them on their way out the door, 'and make sure you're home before four. The priest is coming to read the sutras.'

Left alone, the two sisters began going through a pile of their mother's belongings that Satsuki hadn't got around to looking at. They pulled out old letters, photo albums and postcards, dusted them off and pored over them.

The albums were full of black-and-white photographs from the decades between the First and Second World War. As they flipped the pages, fresh-faced schoolgirls in uniforms, with names such as *Matsuko*, *Fujiko*, *Ayako* and *Tomiko* written neatly beside the photos, stared calmly out at them. When they got to the end without having found anyone they recognised, not even their mother, it dawned on them that the album must have belonged to their aunt.

Next they came across a man's dress kimono, which presumably had belonged to their mother's elder brother, and, more surprising still, an envelope stuffed with discoloured photographs of even more ancient and uncertain vintage, full of people and scenery completely unfamiliar to them. They also found old postcards and letters sent from some long-forgotten warfront written in beautiful but illegible calligraphy.

Satsuki thought she had cleared out the house quite thoroughly after her mother's death. But going over it again now she was amazed at how much clutter remained. At this rate, she remarked only half-jokingly to her sister, she wouldn't be surprised if some old correspondence between their Uncle Teruyuki and the understated beauty turned up. But nothing of the kind did.

Instead, at around two o'clock in the afternoon, the back gate opened and a woman sauntered into the garden.

'Good afternoon!' she greeted them, sitting down on the edge of the veranda, adding, in a somehow incongruously cheerful voice, 'I heard that if I came by today everyone would be here.' She looked at Satsuki. 'Is that you, Satchan? And you must be Kayo. My, but haven't you two grown!' she observed a bit idiotically, as though they were teenagers rather than married women in their thirties and forties. Moreover – and strangest of all – one might have been forgiven for thinking she was younger than either of them. 'I heard your dear mother, Kimiyo, passed away,' she said. 'You must let me pay my respects.'

Rising to her feet, the woman glided into the house and went straight over to the altar. Kneeling, she lit a stick of incense, then picked up the little brass bell and rang it once before placing her palms together and bowing her head. Satsuki noticed she wasn't carrying so much as a purse or a small handbag, though if she lived in the neighbourhood perhaps it wasn't surprising. She wore a long navy skirt, from which protruded a pair of astonishingly white calves, as though she had never been out in the sun.

'Were you Uncle Teruyuki's girlfriend?' asked Kayo.

'Yes,' the woman replied simply, not the least embarrassed by the question. Then, glancing down at the album open on the floor in front of Satsuki and Kayo, she let out a gasp. 'Well, I'll be!' She began slowly turning the pages and poring over the photographs. Watching her, Satsuki and Kayo sensed that the faces that had meant nothing to them were coming to life before her eyes. Then, turning the page to a picture of their Uncle Teruyuki in his younger days, her hand paused in midair.

'Have you had any news of our uncle?' asked Kayo. 'To tell the truth, our family has lost touch with him.'

'No – he hasn't written to me in ages!' the woman replied. 'I think he's forgotten all about me ... I should have married Teruyuki when I had the chance – if I had, he wouldn't have gone off to Brazil!' She said this as though trying to convince herself that it was true.

'What do you mean, "when you had the chance"?'

'The time he proposed to me, before he met ... that other person.'

'Did he?'

'Yes, but I turned him down. So he went and married her instead ... But really, I didn't have a choice in the matter. You see, it had already been decided I was to marry someone else.'

Kayo and Satsuki exchanged confused looks, taken aback by this sudden twist in what had seemed a straight-forward love story.

'Teruyuki seemed to be of two minds,' she continued. 'I didn't know he was madly in love with me. He said it would be my fault if he married someone else and went to Brazil ... In any case, I wouldn't have made him a good wife. He was better off...'

Breaking off in mid-sentence, the woman's eyes fell on the bright orange hozuki hanging over the Obon altar, as though noticing it for the first time.

'Are they empty?' she asked. 'The pods – is there fruit inside?' She explained how, as a little girl, she would remove the berries and blow into the empty pod, making a sound like a croaking frog.

As she looked at the woman's profile, Satsuki began to have the feeling that she had met her before, though perhaps it was only her imagination...

'You slowly massage the fruit inside the pod like this,' the woman was saying, 'until the colour darkens. Then, when it's all soft and mushy, you use a toothpick to make a hole in the husk and ease it out. Next you rinse it so it's all nice and clean, then put your mouth to the hole and blow...'

'Oh, what a fun day! I can't remember the last time I enjoyed myself so much,' the woman exclaimed as she was leaving. The tea and sweets Kayo had put out on the table for her remained untouched.

A bit later, Kayo's husband arrived by car from Tokyo.

'Doesn't the air feel fresh out here in the country!' Atsushi said, inhaling deeply. 'And it's so much cooler, even though we're not that far from Tokyo!' Being from a Christian family in Kobe, he told Satsuki excitedly, he had never celebrated a proper Obon. 'Look what I brought,' he said proudly, as he unloaded beer and a shopping bag full of snack food from the car.

'Dried squid? Salami?' his wife exclaimed, inspecting the contents. 'What are you thinking, dear? We can't eat meat or fish during Obon! This will have to go in the cupboard until later,' she said, confiscating the contraband.

'Huh? You mean we aren't going to have a barbecue?' he said, looking genuinely pained.

Just then, Masaru, Ayumi and Tsutomu returned from their outing to the river and reported that they had run into a group of children about their age and had a wonderful time. Soon Kayo began chivvying everyone to get ready, saying the priest would be arriving at four o'clock, and got the children changed into fresh clothes. Tsutomu was already starting to yawn by this point and looked as though he would nod off the moment the priest began reciting the sutras.

More than ten minutes ahead of the scheduled time, the priest bounded up to the front door in high spirits.

'So few people take the trouble of having the sutras recited at home these days,' he said. 'Everyone moves around so much, even out here in the countryside. Coming all this way to observe Obon, as you have, shows great piety. It gladdens the heart.'

And with that he began intoning the sutras with gusto and at great length, and followed it up with a long-winded sermon. By the end, not only Tsutomu was fast asleep but Ayumi too, and even their father and uncle were both nodding their heads as they struggled to remain conscious.

To no one's surprise, the priest's sermon was a lamentation on how the true meaning of Obon was being lost. Obon, he explained, derived from the Sanskrit word *ullambana*, meaning 'hanging upside down,' one of the torments of Hell. He related how Maudgalyayana, a disciple of the Buddha, upon learning that his dead mother was in Hell, asked his teacher how to save her. The Buddha instructed him to prepare 'plentiful offerings of food and drink' and pray for his mother's soul.

'Such is the story as it is known among the general population today,' said the priest. 'Yet what people fail to grasp is that Obon is celebrated on the fifteenth day of the seventh lunar month for a reason: that was when, in the Buddha's day, monks broke their long period of meditation and fasting. The Buddha, then, was telling Maudgalyayana to feed the hungry monks and pray that the merit accrued through this pious act be transferred to his mother. Maudgalyayana did so, and his mother was reborn in paradise.'

The priest spoke so passionately and repeatedly about the 'plentiful offerings of food and drink' that Satsuki and Kayo realised that he intended to stay for dinner.

Kayo had put great effort into that night's meal. Her child-friendly menu included an eclectic but carefully considered array of dishes: vinegared rice balls in fried tofu pockets; sushi rolls with strips of reconstituted dried gourd; sautéed aubergine and capsicum in miso sauce; chilled tomato slices with onion and soy sauce vinaigrette; and, her pièce de résistance, a boiled vegetable salad of carrots, spinach, wild mountain plants, and yam cake in a sesame-tofu dressing. But after all her effort, she was forced to look on in horror, if not surprise, as her offspring licked off the sesame-tofu dressing and left the vegetables on their plates.

Having eaten his fill, the priest looked up from his empty plate with a contented expression and his eye fell on the Obon altar that the two sisters and the children had decorated that afternoon.

'As long as I'm here,' he said, 'shall we make the traditional offering to the hungry ghosts?'

'The hungry ghosts?' repeated Kayo, puzzled.

'When the ancestral spirits return home at Obon,' he explained, 'they are accompanied by souls we call "hungry ghosts". A devout Buddhist visits their loved ones' graves every year on their death anniversaries and at the vernal and autumnal equinoxes. But many departed ones have nobody in this world to pray for them or to make offerings at their graves. These neglected souls cannot swallow normal food because their throats are swollen from hunger. Hence, they must be given washed, uncooked rice mixed with chopped raw vegetables.'

'Can these hungry souls enter any house?' asked Satsuki.

'Anywhere there is food for them to eat ... But as

this practice is dying out, in time there may be nowhere for them to go. As priests, this is one of many things we worry about. Thankfully, you have been so good as to come here today because of your connection to this house, so we are able to offer them a bit of the feast you have prepared.'

Satsuki got up and went to the kitchen. She rinsed a cup of uncooked rice in the sink and diced some vegetables. Putting these together on a plate, she took it to the Obon altar. When she had finished making the offering, the priest bowed deeply and said that he looked forward to speaking with her later about the arrangements for the family grave. Then, with a look of great satisfaction, he took the donation envelope Satsuki discreetly proffered him and left.

'To hear that priest tell it,' said Atsushi sarcastically, 'you'd think this was a day for feeding him and his hungry ghosts.'

'It does make you look at Obon in a new light, doesn't it?' his wife quipped back.

That night, the conversation turned back yet again to the understated beauty.

'She came back today, as promised,' said Kayo.

'Quite the mystery woman,' added Satsuki.

'Hey, shall we look for a picture of her in that old album?' suggested Masaru.

'Are you really so fascinated by her beauty?' said Satsuki.

'It's not her beauty,' said her husband, 'but her general *existence* that fascinates me.'

'For me it's her beauty,' said Atsushi, bringing over the album. 'I want to have a look.'

But search as they might, they could find no picture of the woman.

THE NEXT MORNING, Satsuki went to the storage room and got out the special mixing bowl, rolling pin, and pastry board for making udon.

When they were children, their mother, then still relatively young, had often made udon for them, as she had learned from her mother. But it was taxing on the arms and back and there came a time when she had to stop.

Satsuki had found the udon-making set during a search of the old house after her mother passed away but she had never got around to using it. Today would probably be the first and the last time. In this part of Gunma an udon rolling pin was considered an essential accoutrement to any household and part of every bride's trousseau. As for the red-and-black lacquer mixing bowl, judging from its age, it would seem to have belonged not to their mother but to their grandmother.

Satsuki first washed the implements, which were covered in dust, then put them out on the veranda to dry. In the afternoon, she set to work.

The children were greatly intrigued by the whole process, which Ayumi deemed a suitable subject for inclusion in her summer essay. And since the two husbands, who had nothing else to do, also showed a keen interest, Satsuki gave them a kilo of flour and put them to work mixing and kneading the dough.

The flour had been purchased at the local supermarket on the way home from the flower market the day before. The words *Grown and milled in Gunma* were printed on the package. Apparently, this beige-ish-coloured flour was the secret to making authentic udon. Their mother had always complained that the flour sold in Tokyo wasn't fit to eat.

The ingredients of udon were simply flour, water and salt. Kayo had gone and dug out the time-honoured family recipe, which she had got her mother to write down for her back in primary school when she had to do a homework assignment on 'My Taste of Home' or something to that effect. The flour and water were combined in a ratio of slightly less than two to one then mixed to a shaggy consistency. Then the dough was kneaded until it stuck together and could be rolled into a ball. Lastly, it was placed inside a double-layered plastic bag and kneaded some more underfoot.

On the veranda, the two husbands and two children took turns stomping on the bag of dough, a spectacle that elicited much laughter from the sisters, who snapped photos, while passers-by paused to peer over the hedge to see what all the merriment was about. Occasionally, some old codger, unable to resist putting in his two pennyworth, would call over the hedge and tell them to knead harder or turn the dough over.

Only after the dough had been thoroughly kneaded, formed again into a ball, and allowed to rest for an hour was it ready to be rolled out. Rolling out the dough took considerable strength, a task beyond five-year-old Tsutomu, who clamoured to be allowed a go as the two husbands took turns with the rolling pin, leaning over the pastry board with the boy under their arms. Satsuki, as she dusted flour over the rolled-out disks of dough and then folded and cut them into neat strips with her niece, recalled standing beneath her mother's own arms and watching her roll out the dough. Then Kayo gathered up the strips of dough into fist-sized bundles, wound them into nests, and laid them out in rows on the pastry board. In Satsuki's mind, her sister in her red apron overlapped with an image of their late aunt in her long-sleeved white smock.

Surveying the little scene around her, it occurred to Satsuki that the belief that the ancestral spirits returned at Obon wasn't something mystical or paranormal, nor was it a metaphor for human existence – it was an expression of how the dead were resurrected through the gestures and actions of the living in the performance of traditional customs and practices. And just as this realisation crossed Satsuki's mind, a slightly bent figure in a lavender kimono made of silk gauze, tied with a linen obi, appeared beneath the Obon lanterns hanging over the garden gate, causing Satsuki to catch her breath.

'Mum!' she blurted out.

Kayo stopped what she was doing. Pushing her glasses onto her nose, she squinted in the direction of Satsuki's gaze.

'So it is.'

'Huh?'

The husbands also looked up in shocked disbelief as a woman bearing a striking resemblance to their late mother-in-law, and dressed in one of her favourite kimonos, sank down on the edge of the veranda, apparently exhausted.

'My, what a journey!' she exclaimed. 'Some water, please!'

'Sis, is that you?' said Kayo, returning from the kitchen with a glass of water.

'Of course, it's me. What did you think?' said the woman.

'Well, I mean, you're wearing Mum's kimono.'

'It's the only decent summer one I've got.'

'And the sash. That's Mum's, too.'

'It's the only one that matches.'

'We didn't think you were coming. Shouldn't you be in Samezu?'

'Yes, don't worry. The big cleaning is done and my duties there are over. Tomoharu's only the youngest of three sons, after all ... Anyway, I couldn't miss Mother's last Obon, now could I?' With this, she got up from the veranda and came into the house. 'Oh, you're making udon!' she said, practically licking her lips. 'What a treat!' It was uncanny how similar in appearance she was to their mother at that age.

'Isn't Tomoharu with you?'

'You needn't concern yourself with *him* – he's got his own troubles.'

'So how did things go in Samezu?'

'Oh, just a lot of bickering over the old man's estate and who gets what – as one would expect. In the end, they divvied it up according to the will. You should've heard

Tomoharu's brothers complaining! Serves them right for not sitting down and discussing things properly with their father before he died. Of course, most of the inheritance is tied up in the family business, which goes to the eldest, as is only natural. Tomoharu hardly gets a penny.'

The arrival of Fumie pulled them all suddenly back to the real world, with all its petty concerns and grievances.

The pot of water on the stove had begun bubbling away. Into it they dropped the freshly cut noodles, unravelling the bundles as they did so, then lowered the flame as foam began to rise to the edge of the pot. After about eight minutes, the noodles were transferred to a bowl of ice water to firm them up. Once drained, the plump noodles glistened invitingly in the strainer.

'Don't be ridiculous!' roared Fumie when Kayo began fussing about making the dipping sauce from fish broth, saying it wouldn't be vegetarian. 'The ancestors haven't come all this way for a second-rate meal. Hurry up and make it before the noodles are ruined!' And, taking an old smock out of a drawer and pulling it on over her kimono, she took up her position in the kitchen, looking even more like their mother than before. The expression 'living image' popped into Satsuki's mind, though it wasn't one she normally used.

Minutes later, the dining table was covered with bamboo baskets full of glistening noodles, steaming bowls of fish broth and small dishes of steamed spinach. For garnish there was ground sesame seed, shredded dried seaweed, grated ginger and strips of fried tofu. In addition, Kayo had prepared a colourful assortment of vegetable tempura to be eaten with the noodles. It was a feast worthy of the many people who in the past had gathered around that very table: grandparents, parents, aunts and uncles who had since died or fallen out of touch, and distant relatives whose names no one remembered.

'Say, Sis,' said Satsuki, suddenly thinking of something. 'Did you know Aunt Kaido once had a daughter?'

'You mean Yoko?'

'So it's true, then.'

'She was two or three years younger than me,' said Fumie. 'She drowned in the river, poor thing.'

'And do you remember Yohei, the son of the tofu-maker?'

'The one who became an imported car dealer?'

'Wow, Sis – you know everything!'

'I heard that he died.'

'Well, you've got that part wrong. He's alive and kicking. As a matter of fact, he dropped by the day before yesterday.'

'Is that so? I heard he'd married, sold the tofu shop and moved far away. You mean to say he still comes back for Obon?'

'He told me it'd been eight years since his last visit. But what made you think he was dead?'

'I remember hearing about it while Mother was still alive.'

Fumie had never seemed at all close to their late mother. And yet it appeared that she had absorbed a good deal of family gossip over the years, if only by virtue of being the eldest sibling.

Just then Satsuki and Kayo seemed to have the same thought: *If anyone knew, Fumie would.*

'What about Uncle Teruyuki?' they blurted out in unison.

'Mother's younger brother? You've got me there. No one's heard a peep out of him in years.'

'Yes, but what about his ex-girlfriend?'

'The one who jilted him?'

'Yes.'

'Her name was Tokie. She died too.'

'There you go again! You can't go killing off everyone like that, Sis. We saw her just yesterday – she dropped by to offer incense.'

'Now that *is* odd,' said Fumie. 'After Uncle Teruyuki married, she broke off all contact with our family. Then she too eventually married and moved away.'

'Well, it seems she got divorced, or was widowed, and moved back.'

'What rubbish. If she had, Mother would have heard about it.'

'Maybe it was after Mum died,' said Satsuki. 'By the way, how old do you suppose she'd be now?'

'Tokie? Let's see ... if Mother were still alive she'd be seventy-two. Uncle Teruyuki was eight years younger, so that would make him sixty-four. My guess is Tokie would be around sixty ... mid- to late-fifties at best, I suppose.'

Masaru shook his head. Kayo and Satsuki fell silent.

'What is it?' asked Fumie. 'What's wrong?'

'Nothing,' said Satsuki. 'So she's older than you then?'

'Of course! What did you think?' Fumie shot back indignantly. But if she had been there yesterday, she would have understood: the woman they had come to call the 'understated beauty' had not looked a day over forty-five.

You slowly massage the fruit inside like this ... when it's all soft and mushy, you use a toothpick to ease it out ... then put your mouth to the hole and blow...

Satsuki had decided Tokie had indeed been the older girl she remembered teaching her that trick as a child, but the maths didn't add up. How was one to explain it? A thought began to form in her mind, not unlike the one her husband had expressed, but it was so absurd she dismissed it immediately.

Early the next morning Fumie set off for Tokyo. Before leaving she said: 'You concentrate on preparing for your trip, Satchan. Don't worry about the grave or the altar. Somehow, I'll look after them while you're in South Africa. Anyway, Tomoharu and I will be up again soon to go through the house one last time and get rid of anything we don't need. I'd like you to be there, too.'

Exchanging amused glances at these peremptory parting words, Satsuki and Kayo watched their elder sister leave.

As soon as they had finished packing up, Kayo and her family piled into the car, her husband climbing behind the wheel. They were heading into the thick of the holiday traffic but Atsushi said they would be fine so long as they avoided the expressway. 'Don't worry,' he declared confidently, 'I'll get us home in no time.'

And so it was left to Satsuki and Masaru to see the ancestral spirits back to the family grave one final time.

Can we come again next year, Mum? Can we – please? Tsutomu had begged his mother as they were getting into the car. *I'm afraid we can't, dear, the house won't be here.* But her answer had not satisfied the little boy. *We have to! I promised I'd come back!*

His mother tried reasoning with him. 'Next year Uncle Masaru can play with you at home—'

'Not Uncle Masaru!' the boy said, speaking over her. '*Yoko!*'

'Yoko – who's Yoko?'

'The girl I was playing with! Can we come back, Mum? Can we?'

'I'm sorry, dear. But I told you, this house won't be here.'

'But we have to! I promised!'

Satsuki's nephew had gone on and on in this vein until the car door shut and she could no longer hear his voice. Then the car pulled away and she waved goodbye, not quite sure whether she had heard Tsutomu correctly. Had he really said he had played with a girl named Yoko?

'Dear, didn't you say Masaru and Ayumi played with some children down by the river?' she asked, turning to her husband.

'Yes, several.'

'Was there a little girl about Tsutomu's age?'

'Let's see ... Yes, I think so.'

Was her name Yoko? she wanted to ask. But she felt she couldn't. Nor did she need to.

'Let's go,' she said instead, lighting the portable paper lantern from one of the pair on the altar. As they set off for the temple, up ahead of them Satsuki saw an old woman, also carrying a lantern, walking slowly in the direction of the temple.

So ended their last Obon.

Original Publications

Translated by Ian McCullough MacDonald

'Things Remembered and Things Forgotten'
(おぼえていること、忘れてしまったこと) first published
in *Granta Japan with* 早稲田文学 01, Wasedabungaku,
2014. English translation first published in
Granta 127, 2014.

'Global Positioning System' (全地球測位システム)
first published in *The Long Goodbye* (長い別れ),
Bungeishunju, 2015.

'Kirara's Paper Plane' (きらりの紙飛行機) first published
in *Ghost* (ゴースト), Asahi Shimbun, 2017.

'Childhood Friends' (おさななじみ) first published in
Wonderful View (眺望絶佳), Kadokawa Bunko, 2012.

'The Last Obon' (最後のお盆) first published in
Coming Of Age (冠・婚・葬・祭), Chikuma Shobo, 2016.

Translated by Ginny Tapley Takemori

'When My Wife Was a Shiitake' (妻が椎茸だったころ)
and 'The Pet Civet' (ハクビシンを飼う) first published in
When My Wife Was a Shiitake (妻が椎茸だったころ),
Kodansha, 2013. The English translation of 'When My

Wife Was a Shiitake' was previously published in Words Without Borders, 2015.

'The Life Story of a Sewing Machine' (ミシンの履歴) and 'The Harajuki House' (原宿の家) first published in *Ghost* (ゴースト), Asahi Shimbun, 2017.

'A Special Day' (今日はなんだか特別な日) first published in *Wonderful View* (眺望絶佳), Kadokawa Bunko, 2012.

SORT OF BOOKS would like to thank Saho Baldwin and Madoka Hanajiri of Bungeishunju Ltd for their generous help in granting and obtaining permissions for this English language edition.

THE TRANSLATORS

IAN MCCULLOUGH MACDONALD grew up near
Washington, D.C. and holds a doctorate in Japanese
literature from Stanford. He has translated novels, short
stories and history, including *The Curious Casebook of
Inspector Hanshichi* and the Agatha Christie Award-
winning *The Black Cat Takes a Stroll*. He lives in Singapore.

GINNY TAPLEY TAKEMORI has translated fiction by more
than a dozen early modern and contemporary Japanese
authors. Her translation of Sayaka Murata's *Convenience
Store Woman* was awarded the 2020-2021 Lindsley and
Masao Miyoshi Prize. Her translations of Kyoko Nakajima's
The Little House was published in February 2019, and
Sayaka Murata's *Earthlings* in 2020. She lives in Japan.